# Miracle Muffins!

# Miracle Muffins!

## Amazingly Delicious
## Treats Without
## All That Fat

PATTY NEELEY

Prima Publishing

© 1996 by Patty Neeley

PRIMA PUBLISHING and colophon are registered trademarks of Prima Communications, Inc.

Library of Congress Cataloging in Publication Data

Neeley, Patty Ann.
Miracle muffins:amazingly delicious treats without all that fat!
/by Patty Neeley.
p.    cm.
Includes index.
ISBN 0-7615-0423-0
1. Muffins.    2. Low-fat diet—Recipes.    I. Title.
TX770.M83N44    1996
641.8'15—dc20                                           96-23134
                                                                    CIP


96 97 98 99 00 AA 10 9 8 7 6 5 4 3 2 1
Printed in the United States of America

## HOW TO ORDER

Single copies may be ordered from Prima Publishing, P.O. Box 1260BK, Rocklin, CA 95677; telephone (916) 632-4400. Quantity discounts are also available. On your letterhead, include information concerning the intended use of the books and the number of books you wish to purchase.

Visit us online at http://www.primapublishing.com

To my husband,

RANDY STAHLBERGER,

for his ever constant
love and support.

# CONTENTS

## Fruity Muffins 35

## Savory Muffins 51

PART TWO

# Other Heavenly Treats

Contents

# Hotcakes and Waffles 109

# Syrups, Toppings, and Spreads 121

Contents

# SPECIAL THANKS

*To Prima Publishing* You guys are the best! Thank you once again for your fantastic teamwork and your dedication to excellence. I am very fortunate to work with such a great group!

*To my editor Georgia Hughes* Thank you again for all of your support and hard work.

*To Leslie Yarborough* Leslie, I want to extend a very heartfelt thanks to you for making not only my first experience with the editing process easier to handle, but this one as well. Your patience and dedication to your work are highly appreciated!

*To all of my friends and family* Thank you, thank you for your support and encouragement, as well as for so diligently disposing of all those muffins! I can't even begin to say how much I appreciate and love all of you and how grateful I am for your belief in my dreams. It is because of you that I am able to work so hard. I am one very lucky gal!

# INTRODUCTION

Rise and shine, sleepyhead! Roll yourself out of that bed and reach for the sky. . . . That's right—enjoy a big yawn and take a good, long stretch. . . . Now, what's for breakfast? . . . What's that? Not enough time for breakfast? You don't bother with breakfast? You're on a diet? Nonsense! That grumbling stomach is trying to tell you something; breakfast is the most important meal of the day! Now I know in this day and age, it's a little far-fetched to expect to sit down every morning to the traditional breakfast ensemble of coffee, juice, toast, cereal, eggs, and so on, but that doesn't mean you should skip breakfast altogether. Don't start your morning off with a stone-cold furnace: Fire that baby up!

Perhaps you're bored with the usual quick choices: cold cereal, breakfast bars, last night's pizza, or—worst of all—those fattening doughnuts, Danish, muffins, and the like that somehow manage to win out over everything else. Well, listen up, because I'm about to offer you so many deliciously healthy alternatives that you'll find yourself going to bed early every night simply because you can't wait to have breakfast the next morning!

Imagine yourself waking up to the smell of fresh brewed coffee and the sensuous taste of a Bear Claw Muffin with its crispy streusel topping and rich, moist interior. Or maybe you would prefer an Old-Fashioned Scone, piping hot and oozing with sweet raspberry jam. And for those lazy weekend mornings when you actually have time to enjoy yourself, think about diving into a stack of luscious Lemon Poppy-Seed Hotcakes, drizzled with warm raspberry syrup. Got a real hearty appetite? How about some Chocolate Chip Hotcakes, swimming in gooey Caramel Pecan Syrup?

Don't go away just yet—there's more. The choices are seemingly endless: You can enjoy slice upon slice of moist breakfast breads and coffee cakes such as Cranberry Rhubarb Bread or the absolutely addictive Apricot Lemon Tea Bread. Or dig into mounds of muffins, created with every flavor in mind from the fruitiest blueberry to such savory delights as Sweet Corn and Roasted Red Pepper Muffins and Sun-Dried Tomato and Rosemary Muffins.

I know exactly what you're thinking, can this be true? Can there be so many delicious goodies to indulge in, without indulging in excess fat and calories as well? My answer to you is an enthusiastic yes! I was notorious for skipping breakfast, and inevitably, when I did give in to my growling stomach, I had little concern for the consequences that those doughnuts would inevitably deliver. Something had to change and it was not going to be my passion for sweets! This was the perfect motivation to inspire me to create those flavor combinations that I just can't seem to live without, and put them into a wide assortment of breakfast treats, while simultaneously cutting back on calories and fat grams. Sure, some days an honest to goodness butterhorn Danish may win out, but it's wonderful to have delicious and healthy options for all those other days.

This book not only offers some deliciously healthy breakfast alternatives, but some creative options for other special occasions. Many of the recipes are perfect for brunch, afternoon tea, or any other social gathering you can think of. You will also want to serve many of the savory muffins with lunchtime soups and salads and in place of the usual bread with dinner. And to add to the fun, there's a chapter full of mouthwatering syrups and spreads just waiting to be matched up with any of the goodies in this book. . . .

Ready for something special? Well, what are you waiting for? Better get into that kitchen; a delicious, healthy breakfast is only a few steps away!

# Equipment, Ingredients, and Helpful Baking Tips

The recipes in this book are delicious, but you'll find that they're neither difficult nor time-consuming to make! If muffins, coffee cakes, and other breakfast treats were, we'd never get breakfast at all—by the time it was ready, we'd be too busy with lunch. Nevertheless, no matter how short and sweet a recipe may be, you'll find that the right equipment, the right ingredients, and the right techniques always come in handy.

## Equipment

The equipment requirements for this particular book are not at all elaborate; however, proper equipment is always important no matter what you are baking or cooking. You don't have to have the most expensive equipment available, but be sure that what you do have is sturdy and dependable. The following list describes some of the equipment and utensils needed for the recipes in this book.

## ELECTRIC MIXER

There are only a few recipes in this entire book that require the use of an electric mixer. If you don't have a stand mixer, a simple hand mixer works just as well.

## FOOD PROCESSOR

If you are at all serious about cooking or baking, then you know that it is next to impossible to try and get by without a food processor. There are several recipes in this book that depend on one for chopping or pureeing. You do not have to have a top-of-the-line model, or even a full-sized one for that matter, especially if you only use it for small tasks or aren't cooking for very many. These days, many food processors that are smaller than the standard size are available. These are, however, larger than the mini choppers, and the two should not be confused. The food processor I use is the Cuisinart Little Pro Plus. With a capacity of about four cups, it has all the power and performance of the large models, yet takes up half the space. Any good quality brand will work fine for this book.

## BAKING PANS

Your pans are literally the foundation for your culinary creations, whether they're cooked, baked, simmered, or stewed. Remember, using cheap flimsy equipment or the wrong equipment at the wrong time is courting disaster.

For the lower-fat recipes in this book, I had the best luck with glass, Pyrex, and heavier aluminum bakeware. I found that nonstick aluminum bakeware didn't work well; everything I baked in it was very susceptible to burning. For the muffins, you will need aluminum muffin pans. Because the majority of the recipes make fourteen to sixteen muffins, two pans are ideal: one that sleeps twelve and one half-pan that sleeps six. For the coffee cakes and tea breads, you'll need an 8 × 8 × 2-inch deep square baking pan, at least two 8 × 3¾-inch loaf pans, and an 8 × 2-inch deep round pan. You will also need a 9 × 13-inch baking dish, and an 8-inch round bundt or tube type baking pan.

## COOKIE SHEETS

As mentioned above, nonstick bakeware does not work well for the recipes in this book. You'll get far better results from a heavy aluminum sheet pan. If you have access to a restaurant supply store, you would be well off to purchase what is called an aluminum half sheet pan. These are a bit larger than the cookie sheets that you find for home use, and they are far less likely to warp. One of these should last forever.

## WIRE WHISK

I consider the whisk one of the most indispensable tools in my kitchen. I have several of them, ranging in size from small to quite large. You don't have to have a whisk collection, but you really should have at least one good wire whisk. You'll find that an elongated whisk is the most versatile and appreciate the convenience of being able to switch to a smaller bowl without switching to a smaller whisk. Don't buy a cheap, flimsy one with all of four wires on it. Go to a shop that sells quality cookware and pick up a stainless steel elongated balloon whisk that is approximately 8 inches long starting at the base of the wires. The whisk itself should have no fewer than eight wires. This is the size that I used while preparing the recipes in this book and it worked perfectly for every task.

## SAUCEPANS

Always use heavier bottomed pans for better heat conductivity. You will be less likely to scorch a mixture. If you don't want to invest in professional-style cookware, which is made of anodized steel, stainless steel is one of the best ways to go. Enamel-coated cast-iron pans are also a good choice.

## MIXING BOWLS

I like stainless steel mixing bowls the best, usually one large-and one medium-sized one. Glass or Pyrex bowls are also fine. When you use a whisk or are a hand-held mixer, other types of bowls, especially ceramic or pottery ones, don't fare too well. The spinning beaters can really damage them. I won't be too strict about mixing bowls for this book; most of the time you will be combining ingredients in them with either your hands or a rubber spatula.

## OVEN THERMOMETER

For those of us who happen to own an inaccurate oven, an oven thermometer is indispensable. These thermometers are priced around ten dollars and well worth the investment. Designed to sit on your oven floor or hang from one of the racks, an oven thermometer will give you an accurate reading of the internal temperature of your oven.

## FINE-MESH SIEVE

There are a few recipes in this book that require a fine-mesh sieve. The wire mesh in these sieves is much finer than that of a standard wire strainer. This is a must when straining fresh berry purees since only the precious juice and pulp can pass through, leaving everything else behind. Fine-mesh sieves are also the best thing for dusting cakes and the like with a delicate coating of powdered sugar or cocoa.

## NONSTICK GRIDDLE

Please resist all urges to use the household frying pan, especially the one that's begun to warp and sink in the middle. If you use a frying pan, invest in one that is heavy-duty cast iron or anodized steel, flat and shallow, and as large in circumference as your burner can accommodate. This is not the ideal way to make your pancakes since you can often make only one large pancake or two smaller ones at a time, but nevertheless, it works. However, if you don't mind investing a little in a piece of worthwhile equipment, I strongly suggest purchasing a cast-iron griddle made for the stove top. This is the ideal pancake tool and is as close to what the restaurants use as you're going to get at home. If you are one of the lucky ones, you already have Grandma's or even Great Grandma's old cast-iron griddle with its smooth nonstick surface that has been seasoned perfectly from years of use. Your pancakes must be divine! For those of you less fortunate, do not despair. You can buy a griddle without spending too much money. I paid less than $15.00 for mine. It is a nice, heavy cast-iron design that measures around 18 inches long and 9 inches wide. It sits perfectly across two stove burners, which gives me plenty of space to flip those hotcakes—more than one at a time!—and it is not so big that I'm left wondering where in the heck to put it when it's not in use. If you buy one, be sure to read the instructions on seasoning the griddle before you actually use it. This crucial step creates the classic nonstick surface that is synonymous with cast ironware. There are, of course, griddles made with a nonstick surface such as Teflon. These are also wonderful to use, though they do cost more than the plain cast iron.

## WAFFLE IRON

If you don't already own an electric waffle iron, you can purchase one at almost any department store. Be sure to shop around since prices vary quite a bit from store to store. Waffle irons come in all different shapes and sizes, from the traditional large round Belgian style with four divided sections to a square version. I have even seen waffle irons that make heart-shaped waffles! You can choose one that will best suit your needs and the size of your family. I have a nice compact model made by Oster that makes two perfect 4-inch-square waffles at a time, and then folds up neatly so I can stash it under the cupboard.

## PARCHMENT PAPER

Parchment paper, which is designed to hold up to the heat of an oven, is what the professionals use instead of aluminum foil for lining cookie sheets and cake pans. I happen to love it because it's easier to use than foil and it doesn't tear when you use a spatula to remove something, but for the recipes in this book, aluminum foil will work fine. I have found that parchment paper is not all that easy to come by, and when you do happen to find it in a store, it is only sold in rolls. These are obnoxious, since you need to cut the paper to the proper length and then coax it to lie flat on your sheet or pan. When I worked in restaurants, parchment paper was the only thing I used, but then we were able to get it packaged in nice flat sheets. I have noticed that a few stores are starting to carry it packaged that way, but it is rather expensive. In the end, it's only a matter of preference. Aluminum foil works just fine for the recipes in this book, but if you are used to parchment paper then by all means, stay with it!

## Ingredients

The following is a list of some of the ingredients you'll find in the recipes in this book that need a bit of elaboration to avoid any surprises or misunderstandings.

### ALMOND PASTE
It is very easy to confuse almond paste with marzipan when buying it in the store. Marzipan is almond paste with sugar added, making it ideal for candy making and cake decorations. For the recipes in this book you will need pure almond paste, which is packaged in small rolls or cans.

### ANISE EXTRACT
This extract is made from aniseed, a member of the parsley family. It has a strong licorice flavor.

### BARLEY FLOUR
This is a slightly rough textured flour milled from hulled barley. You can find it at most health food stores, and in the health food section of many supermarkets.

### BUTTER, LIGHT
This is a lighter version of the real thing made with ingredients such as buttermilk and gelatin in order to reduce the amount of calories and fat. Most brands will say that they are not recommended for baking or frying. I found it to be quite satisfactory and had no problems whatsoever using it for the recipes in this book, perhaps because these recipes do not call for large quantities of it. The brands I use are Challenge and Land O Lakes. Each has approximately 50 calories and 6 grams of fat per tablespoon.

## CHERRY PIE FILLING

There are many different brands of canned fruit filling on the market, and the quality and amount of fruit in each varies. If you are as choosy as I am, buy the best quality containing the most fruit. I have found Comstock is an excellent brand.

## GARLIC

There are recipes in this book that call for fresh, minced garlic. This doesn't mean you have to spend hours peeling cloves and mincing them. It is perfectly acceptable to use minced garlic from the jar, which is what I did in devising these recipes. Be sure to buy garlic labeled finely minced rather than chopped. I have found quite a difference between the two depending on the brand that you buy.

## MASA

This finely milled corn has the texture of coarse flour. It is traditionally used for making tamales and tortillas, but I have found it works beautifully for hotcakes, scones, and other baked goods. Cornmeal is roughly milled and is *not* a good substitute for masa.

## NEUFCHÂTEL CHEESE, LIGHT

Neufchâtel cheese is very similar to cream cheese. While not fat free, it is reduced in fat by about one-third and contains 70 calories and 6 grams of fat per ounce. There are many brands of reduced fat cream cheese available, but I prefer Philadelphia Neufchâtel cheese for its quality and creaminess. You may use another brand though, as long as the number of calories and grams of fat are close to those cited above.

## NONSTICK COOKING SPRAY

Beware: Not all nonstick sprays are created equal! I am very specific about which ones to use. It is best to stick with vegetable or canola oil spray since these are completely neutral. They have no added flavorings that could affect the taste of your baked goods. Avoid using butter-flavored sprays or olive oil, and definitely avoid diet sprays.

## PEANUT BUTTER, REDUCED FAT

Many brands of peanut butter are now making a reduced fat product, however not all of them are equal in quality. I have found some to be a bit on the grainy side. Use the creamiest one that you can get your hands on. I prefer Jif because it really is the creamiest!

## RICOTTA CHEESE, LOWFAT

Look for brands containing approximately 70 calories and 3 grams of fat per ¼ cup serving. I find a brand called Precious to be an excellent choice.

## SOUR CREAM, LIGHT

This reduced fat version of regular sour cream contains 40 calories and 2.5 grams of fat per two tablespoon serving. I have found differences in texture and creaminess from brand to brand and I do not recommend the very fat-reduced versions. Be sure to read the nutritional information to make sure the number of calories and grams of fat are close to what is listed above for the best results.

## SULTANAS

Sultanas are raisins made from white grapes rather than the usual dark purple ones. I prefer them for certain recipes because they have a light and fruity flavor.

## SUN-DRIED CHERRIES

You can find these in specialty food shops, and sometimes in the dried fruit section of the grocery store. There are different kinds of cherries, but the most popular are Bing and Royal Anne. The Royal Annes are more tart, while the Bings are sweeter and richer.

## SUN-DRIED TOMATOES

There are a couple of ways that you can purchase these. You can buy them in a bulk dried form, which requires that they be soaked in hot water to rehydrate them before use. You can also buy them in jars, already soft and packed in oil. For the Sun-

Dried Tomato and Rosemary Muffins, it is best to use the oil-packed variety because the recipe depends on the oil content of the tomatoes.

## VANILLA EXTRACT

I must take a stand when it comes to the subject of vanilla extract: Nothing tastes like pure vanilla extract or imparts the same flavor to your baked goodies. So accept no substitutes! The recipes in this book depend on it!

# Helpful Baking Tips

Whether you're making the simplest muffins or tea cakes or the most elaborate cakes and cookies, baking can always be a challenge. No matter who's in the kitchen, good old-fashioned hints still come in handy once in a while. For me, it's often the littlest tip that has ended up making the difference between serving luscious goodies to my family and friends and trekking out to my pygmy goat's pen with an armload of rejects that were unfit for human consumption. (At least the goat was happy!) So I've decided to pass along a few of the tips that have really helped me out. At the beginning of each part or section you'll find hints that are specific to the baked goods in that section. The following are some general baking tips that pertain to most of the recipes in this book.

## MIXING METHODS

I always like to pass along my favorite tip when it comes to the subject of mixing: Always have a wire whisk on hand. Nothing works better to combine the wet ingredients. And a whisk is great for combining the dry ingredients as well, especially when you need to work in such things as brown sugar or spices that may have lumped a bit in the container due to moisture. The trusty whisk will never fail you.

A rubber spatula is also indispensable. When you are combining the wet ingredients with the dry, I have found that a simple rubber spatula is the best tool for the job. It allows total control, helps prevent overmixing, and effortlessly scrapes the bowl completely clean.

## BAKING TEMPERATURE

If you have done a reasonable amount of baking, then you are probably well aware of the problems that an inaccurate oven can pose. Perhaps your oven has a mind of its own and refuses to stay in sync with the numbers on the temperature dial.

Fortunately, help is only an oven thermometer away! These inexpensive devices can make the difference between enjoying the fruits of your labor and deep-sixing them! Unlike many ovens, the trusty oven thermometer will be quite honest in telling you what the internal temperature really is. The rest is up to you: You may have to adjust the dial one way or the other, depending on whether your oven cooks too hot or too cool. Do remember that baking temperatures as well as baking times are only guidelines, especially for those inaccurate ovens. I speak from personal experience because my own oven is a far cry from perfect!

## BAKING TIME

If you look at a recipe and think to yourself, "That's too long of a baking time for my oven—it'll burn for sure!" chances are you're probably right. In the end you need to use your own judgment and to check what you're baking and test for doneness close to the end of the baking time.

## TESTING FOR DONENESS

When choosing a cake tester, pick whatever you feel most comfortable with. This could be anything from an official store-bought cake tester to a toothpick or a bamboo skewer. Personally, I prefer a bamboo skewer not only for its length, but because wet or moist crumbs will grab right on to it. Wire cake testers are so thin and slick that nothing but raw batter will stick to them.

The majority of the time the cake tester will come out dry, obviously indicating that your baking is done. Wet crumbs or batter stuck to the cake tester are a sure indication that more baking time is needed, but there is also a gray area. When only a few moist crumbs are stuck to the cake tester, it is safe to say that the cake is done and further baking might only dry it out. In the end, this is a judgment call on your end, but paying close attention to the signs should assure success.

# PART ONE

# Muffins, Muffins, Muffins!

One of the fastest-growing choices for breakfast in these hectic times is a cup of caffeine in any available form, complemented by a delicious muffin. I happen to know many people who can and do miraculously sustain themselves for the whole morning on caffeine and a muffin. To each his own, I say!

However, some of us may be getting more than we are counting on when we reach for that morning muffin. On average, muffins are very high in calories and fat. I have come across some (whose brand names I won't mention) that pack a walloping 500 calories and 36 grams of fat— each! And of course, these muffins are usually poised for the impulse buyer, strategically displayed very close to the checkout counter and the coffeepot. I don't think very many people actually turn them over to read the nutritional information. The whole grocery store must have heard my exclamations of utter disbelief the first time I did.

Muffins for breakfast are here to stay, so there's no reason why they can't be good for you as well as just plain good. Who needs to start their morning off by consuming three days' worth of fat! It's Miracle Muffins to the rescue. In the next three chapters, you will find a bounty of delicious, lower fat, lower calorie versions of your favorite kinds of muffins, from coffee cake style to fruity and even savory. Whether you're looking for a quick breakfast or an afternoon pick-me-up, these muffins are sure to please.

## Muffin Success

There is far more involved in creating the perfect muffin than meets the eye. I used to think: "It's only a muffin— how hard can it possibly be?" Not any more! After five years of trying shortcuts, I know firsthand how easy it is to mess up muffins simply because I didn't give them the respect they deserve.

I wouldn't say right offhand that turning out respectable muffins is hard. As with any other baked goodies, muffins require discipline about following instructions. The bottom line is no cutting corners. Make no mistake: no matter how short or easy a recipe looks, you can bet that there is a specific method for ensuring the proper taste and texture. The following tips explain how to use the recipes in this book to create deliciously successful lowfat muffins.

## Mixing the Batter

Ask any good baker to tell you the secret to successful muffins and she or he is sure to tell you it's all in the handling of the batter. One of the most common reasons for muffin failure is the tendency to overmix the batter, resulting in tough muffins. I really don't care for a muffin that is tough and overworked.

For the muffin recipes in this book, I have instructed you to mix just until all of the ingredients are moist. Use either a wooden spoon or, better yet, a trusty old rubber spatula, to gently stir or fold the ingredients together only to the point where they have combined, and no further. The batter will be rough and lumpy looking. Don't worry about the lumps—they are part of the magic of muffin making.

Many people get into trouble because they simply can't seem to fight the urge to work out those lumps to achieve a nice smooth batter. I can hardly blame them because, technically, batters are supposed to be smooth and uniform and it becomes habit to make them that way. Muffins are one of the exceptions to the rule, and actually depend on being undermixed for their success.

## Pan Preparation

Every muffin recipe in this book will ask that you lightly coat the paper muffin cups with vegetable or canola oil spray. There is nothing more irritating to me than peeling away the paper of my morning muffin, only to find that half of the muffin has peeled away with it! This is what will happen if you forget to coat the insides of the paper muffin cups. This rule doesn't usually apply to regular muffin recipes: the butter or oil in typical muffin batters allows the muffins to easily release from the papers. But I have found that lower fat muffin batters adhere to the paper like glue, leading to the inevitable peeling away of your muffin.

Now I won't go so far as to say that there haven't been times when I was quite human and just plain forgot to coat the papers, yet the muffins still came loose with great ease. I can't explain this phenomena, so I simply refer to it as a true baking miracle. It is best, however, to avoid playing "Muffin Roulette", so to speak, and just be sure to coat those paper muffin cups every time!

## Filling the Muffin Cups

When I make muffins, I want them to be as big as they can possibly be without having to use a jumbo-sized muffin pan. Long gone are the days of only filling the cups half or three-quarters of the way full. Don't hesitate a bit when I ask you to fill them to the rims. Spoon the batter right up to the tops of the paper muffin cups, or at least very close. I promise your muffins are not going to overflow in the oven. Instead, you'll be more likely to get a nice domed top, which is the way a muffin should look as far as I'm concerned. Who wants to eat a measly little flat-topped muffin? I rest my case.

## Baking Muffins

Baking is the most critical leg of your muffin-making journey. Now that you have so carefully mixed up the perfect muffin batter and spooned it clear to the rims of those nicely coated paper muffin cups, it sure would be a shame to overbake the muffins. Remember that baking times and temperatures are only guidelines to go by.

Generally, muffins are baked at a higher temperature than cakes, anywhere from 375 to 400 degrees Fahrenheit. I used to rebel against this, for fear that my muffins were bound to burn at that high a temperature. It took me a while to get over that fear and understand the reasons for turning up the heat. I won't be too technical here, but they have to do with the composition of the batter and the fact that you are dealing with a very small amount of batter that doesn't rely on thirty or forty minutes of baking time to be done. Not only can muffin batter withstand the higher temperature, the high temperature actually causes the batter to rise and bake more quickly, creating the domed top of the muffin.

## Cooling in the Pan

I have seen many people take their muffins out of the oven and immediately dump them out of the pan onto the counter. I prefer to cool muffins in the pan for a little while before removing them. This helps to lock some of the moisture into the muffin that would otherwise have escaped through steam during the cooling process.

For the recipes in this book I have suggested cooling the muffins in the pan for ten minutes before removing them to cool completely. I chose ten minutes simply because most people only have one muffin pan and would be baking all day if they had to wait until the muffins were completely cool before removing them to reuse their pan for another batch of muffins. But if you have the time or the extra muffin pans, you're more than welcome to cool them completely in the pan.

## Storing in Airtight Containers

When it comes to muffins, I like rectangular Tupperware-style containers the best because they keep your muffins from getting squashed. Otherwise, big Ziploc bags work quite well. And last, but not least, there's the old Saran-Wrap-over-the-plate-of-muffins routine. However, if you have any friends who insist on getting their muffins from the grocery store no matter how many wonderful lowfat muffins you try to send their way, you would be wise to have them give you those nifty little plastic containers that their muffins were packed in. They are easy to wash and can be used over again quite a few times.

# Muffins with Coffee Cake Appeal

# Plain Jaynes

Muffins always seem to be loaded with extra ingredients. But there may be times when you don't want all those frills and thrills. Enter the Plain Jayne muffin, a totally stripped classic with none of the fancy options. Simple and sumptuous!

**16 muffins**

| | |
|---|---|
| 3 cups all-purpose flour | 1/3 cup lowfat ricotta cheese |
| 1 1/4 cups granulated sugar | 3 tablespoons canola oil |
| 3/4 teaspoon salt | 1 large whole egg plus 2 egg |
| 1 tablespoon baking powder | whites |
| 1 teaspoon baking soda | 2 tablespoons vanilla extract |
| 3/4 cup lowfat buttermilk | 5 tablespoons plus 1 teaspoon |
| 3/4 cup 2 percent milk | granulated sugar |

Preheat oven to 375 degrees F. Line a muffin pan with paper muffin cups and lightly coat them with vegetable or canola oil spray.

In a large mixing bowl combine flour, 1 1/4 cups sugar, salt, baking powder, and baking soda. In a separate mixing bowl combine all remaining ingredients except for sugar, and whisk together until smooth. Pour into dry ingredients and mix just until all ingredients are moist.

Spoon batter into prepared muffin cups, filling to the rims, and sprinkle the top of each muffin with 1 teaspoon of the remaining granulated sugar. Bake for approximately 20 minutes. Muffins should be light golden brown, and a cake tester inserted into the center should come out clean.

Cool muffins in pan for 10 minutes before removing to cool completely. Store in an airtight container.

### Each Serving Provides

223 Calories, 16% from Fat, 4 g Fat, 42 g Carbohydrates, 5 g Protein, 71 mg Calcium, 1 g Dietary Fiber, 263 mg Sodium, 16 mg Cholesterol.

# Almond Poppy-Seed Muffins

Almond poppy-seed muffins are almost as popular with the
muffin crowd as their lemon poppy-seed cousins, and, as far as
I'm concerned, they're certainly just as tasty. As delicious as
they are, in their traditional form these pack quite a wallop
when it comes to fat. Fortunately, this lowfat version is
much lighter, and you'll find that it's just as heavenly.

## 14 muffins

| | | | |
|---|---|---|---|
| 3 | tablespoons ground almonds | 2½ | tablespoons poppy seeds |
| 2 | tablespoons granulated sugar | ¾ | cup lowfat buttermilk |
| 1 | tablespoon brown sugar | ¾ | cup 2 percent milk |
| 3 | cups all-purpose flour | ⅓ | cup lowfat ricotta cheese |
| 1¼ | cups granulated sugar | 3 | tablespoons canola oil |
| ¾ | teaspoon salt | 2 | large egg whites |
| 1 | tablespoon baking powder | 1 | tablespoon vanilla extract |
| | | 1 | tablespoon almond extract |

Preheat oven to 375 degrees F. Line a muffin pan with paper muffin cups and lightly coat them with vegetable or canola oil spray.

Combine ground almonds, 2 tablespoons granulated sugar, and brown sugar, and set aside.

In a large mixing bowl combine flour, sugar, salt, baking powder, and poppy seeds. In a separate mixing bowl combine all remaining ingredients and whisk together until smooth. Pour into dry ingredients and mix just until all ingredients are moist.

Spoon into prepared muffin cups, filling to the rims, and sprinkle the top of each muffin with 1½ teaspoons of the almond-sugar mixture. Bake for approximately 20 minutes. Muffins should be light golden brown, and a cake tester inserted into the center should come out clean.

Cool muffins in pan for 10 minutes before removing to cool completely. Store in an airtight container.

## Each Serving Provides

236 Calories, 21% from Fat, 5 g Fat, 42 g Carbohydrates, 5 g Protein,
92 mg Calcium, 1 g Dietary Fiber, 214 mg Sodium, 3 mg Cholesterol.

# Molasses-Oatmeal Muffins

I happen to love those chewy molasses-oatmeal cookies, especially the giant ones! But I only indulge in them on the days when I feel like being bad. The rest of the time I enjoy these muffins, which are quite a worthy substitute.

**15 muffins**

2 1/2 cups all-purpose flour
1/2 cup old-fashioned oats
1/2 cup brown sugar, firmly packed
1/2 cup granulated sugar
1/2 teaspoon salt
1 tablespoon baking powder
1 teaspoon baking soda
1/2 teaspoon ground allspice

1/2 cup lowfat buttermilk
1/2 cup 2 percent milk
1/4 cup lowfat ricotta cheese
1 large whole egg plus 1 egg white
1/2 cup molasses
3 tablespoons canola oil
1 tablespoon vanilla extract

Preheat oven to 375 degrees F. Line a muffin pan with paper muffin cups and lightly coat them with vegetable or canola oil spray.

In a large mixing bowl combine flour, oats, brown sugar, granulated sugar, salt, baking powder, baking soda, and allspice. In a separate mixing bowl combine all remaining ingredients and whisk together until smooth. Pour into dry ingredients and mix just until all ingredients are moist.

Spoon batter into prepared muffin cups, filling to the rims, and bake for approximately 20 minutes. Muffins should be light golden brown, and a cake tester inserted into a center should come out clean.

Cool muffins in pan for 10 minutes before removing to cool completely. Store in an airtight container.

### Each Serving Provides

211 Calories, 17% from Fat, 4 g Fat, 39 g Carbohydrates, 4 g Protein, 75 mg Calcium, 1 g Dietary Fiber, 252 mg Sodium, 17 mg Cholesterol.

# Frosted Gingerbread Muffins

If you are as fond of gingerbread as I am, you will definitely want to give these a try. Now you won't have to wait till you tear down the gingerbread house at Christmastime to enjoy this wonderful treat!

**15 muffins**

2 cups all-purpose flour
1 cup whole wheat flour
½ cup granulated sugar
1 tablespoon baking powder
1 teaspoon baking soda
1 teaspoon salt
½ teaspoon each:
   ground ginger
   ground allspice
   ground cloves
   ground cinnamon
   ground cardamom
   ground nutmeg

¾ cup lowfat buttermilk
½ cup 2 percent milk
⅓ cup lowfat ricotta cheese
¼ cup molasses
3 tablespoons canola oil
1 large whole egg plus 2 egg whites
1 tablespoon vanilla extract

Icing
1½ cups powdered sugar
2 tablespoons orange juice

Preheat oven to 375 degrees F. Line a muffin pan with paper muffin cups and lightly coat them with vegetable or canola oil spray.

In a large mixing bowl combine both flours, sugar, baking powder, baking soda, salt, and ground spices. In a separate mixing bowl combine all remaining ingredients and whisk together until smooth. Pour into dry ingredients and mix just until all ingredients are moist.

Spoon batter into prepared muffin cups, filling to the rims, and bake for approximately 20 minutes. Muffins should be light golden brown, and a cake tester inserted into the center should come out clean.

Cool muffins in pan for 10 minutes before removing to cool completely.

Prepare icing: In a small bowl combine sugar and orange juice and stir until smooth and creamy. Frost the top of each cooled muffin with approximately 1 ½ teaspoons of icing. Store in an airtight container.

### Each Serving Provides

216 Calories, 18% from Fat, 4 g Fat, 40 g Carbohydrates, 5 g Protein, 78 mg Calcium, 2 g Dietary Fiber, 192 mg Sodium, 18 mg Cholesterol.

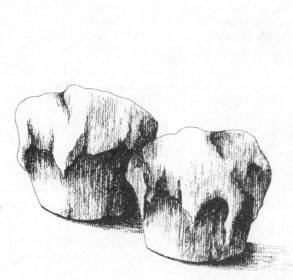

# Cinnamon Streusel Muffins

These are shot full of cinnamon through and through,
especially the crunchy streusel topping. Their rich,
warm taste is perfect with a hot cup of joe!

**12 muffins**

Streusel topping
- 1/3 cup granulated sugar
- 2 tablespoons all-purpose flour
- 1 teaspoon ground cinnamon
- 1 tablespoon light butter, room temperature

Batter
- 2 1/2 cups all-purpose flour
- 1 cup granulated sugar
- 1/2 teaspoon salt
- 1 tablespoon baking powder
- 1 teaspoon baking soda
- 1/4 teaspoon ground cinnamon
- 1/2 cup lowfat buttermilk
- 3/4 cup 2 percent milk
- 2 tablespoons canola oil
- 2 tablespoons light corn syrup
- 1/3 cup lowfat ricotta cheese
- 1 large whole egg plus 2 egg whites
- 1 tablespoon vanilla extract

Preheat oven to 375 degrees F. Line a muffin pan with paper muffin cups and lightly coat them with vegetable or canola oil spray.

Prepare streusel: In a small bowl combine sugar, flour, cinnamon, and butter. Rub mixture together with your fingers to make coarse crumbs and set aside.

Prepare batter: In a large mixing bowl combine flour, sugar, salt, baking powder, baking soda, and cinnamon. In a separate bowl combine all remaining ingredients and whisk together until smooth. Pour into dry ingredients and mix just until all ingredients are moist.

Spoon batter into prepared muffin cups, filling to the rims, and top each muffin with some of the streusel topping. Bake for approximately 20 minutes. Muffins should be light golden brown, and a cake tester inserted into the center should come out clean.

Cool muffins in pan for 10 minutes before removing to cool completely. Store in an airtight container.

Each Serving Provides

249 Calories, 16% from Fat, 5 g Fat, 47 g Carbohydrates, 6 g Protein,
88 mg Calcium, 1 g Dietary Fiber, 307 mg Sodium, 23 mg Cholesterol.

# Peanut Butter Oatmeal Muffins

I created these for my husband, Randy, who is a true peanut
butter freak, and soon discovered that he isn't the only one. I
believe the truth came out after I had polished off my third muffin.

**14 muffins**

| | |
|---|---|
| ³/₄ cup old-fashioned oats | ¹/₂ cup lowfat ricotta cheese |
| 2¹/₄ cups all-purpose flour | 2 large egg whites |
| ¹/₂ cup brown sugar, firmly packed | ¹/₄ cup plus 1 tablespoon reduced fat peanut butter |
| ¹/₂ cup granulated sugar | 1 tablespoon vanilla extract |
| 1 tablespoon baking powder | 2 to 3 tablespoons granulated sugar for tops of muffins |
| 1 teaspoon baking soda | |
| ¹/₂ cup lowfat buttermilk | |
| ³/₄ cup 2 percent milk | |

Preheat oven to 375 degrees F. Line a muffin pan with paper muffin cups and lightly coat them with vegetable or canola oil spray.

Put the oatmeal in a food processor and process it until it is
coarse in texture.

In a large mixing bowl combine oats, flour, ¹/₂ cup granulated
sugar, brown sugar, baking powder, and baking soda. In a separate
mixing bowl combine all the remaining ingredients except for the
granulated sugar, and whisk together until smooth. Pour into the
dry ingredients and mix just until all ingredients are moist.

Spoon batter into prepared muffin cups, filling to the rims,
and sprinkle the top of each muffin with ¹/₂ teaspoon of granulated
sugar. Bake muffins for approximately 20 minutes. Muffins should
be light golden brown, and a cake tester inserted into the center
should come out clean.

Cool in pan for 10 minutes before removing to cool completely. Store in an airtight container.

## Each Serving Provides

206 Calories, 15% from Fat, 4 g Fat, 37 g Carbohydrates, 7 g Protein,
94 mg Calcium, 1 g Dietary Fiber, 217 mg Sodium, 5 mg Cholesterol.

# Maple Bar Muffins

I am a devout fan of maple bars—remember, those bar shaped
doughnuts with the maple icing slathered across the top.
I know that nothing could ever take their place. However, they
can inflict a stiff penalty, especially when eaten in numbers
greater than one! Got a hankering for maple? Try these out—
you will be pleasantly surprised.

**16 muffins**

3 cups all-purpose flour
1 1/4 cups granulated sugar
3/4 teaspoon salt
1 tablespoon baking powder
1 teaspoon baking soda
3/4 cup lowfat buttermilk
3/4 cup 2 percent milk
1/3 cup lowfat ricotta cheese
3 tablespoons canola oil
1 large whole egg plus 2 egg
   whites
2 tablespoons vanilla extract

Maple Icing

1 3/4 cups powdered sugar
1 1/4 teaspoons maple extract
2 tablespoons light Neufchâtel
   cheese, room temperature
1 teaspoon vanilla extract
   pinch of salt
1 tablespoon plus 2 teaspoons
   water

Preheat oven to 375 degrees F. Line a muffin pan with paper muffin cups and lightly coat them with vegetable or canola oil spray.

In a large mixing bowl combine flour, sugar, salt, baking powder, and baking soda. In a separate mixing bowl combine all remaining ingredients and whisk together until smooth. Pour into dry ingredients and mix just until all ingredients are moist.

Spoon batter into prepared muffin cups, filling to the rims, and bake for approximately 20 minutes. Muffins should be light golden brown, and a cake tester inserted into the center should come out clean.

Cool muffins in pan for 10 minutes before removing to cool completely.

Prepare maple icing: Combine all ingredients in a small bowl and beat on medium speed with an electric mixer until creamy and smooth. Frost the top of each cooled muffin with approximately 1 1/2 teaspoons of icing. Store in an airtight container.

### Each Serving Provides

245 Calories, 16% from Fat, 4 g Fat, 46 g Carbohydrates, 5 g Protein, 72 mg Calcium, 1 g Dietary Fiber, 278 mg Sodium, 17 mg Cholesterol.

# Bear Claw Muffins

There's only one pastry that I lust after more than the maple bar, and that is the sinful bear claw. Oh those bear claws! They're so good, but I can't have them as often as I would like, because I'm not willing to suffer the dire consequences. So I came up with the bear claw muffin—this treat dishes up all the delectable flavors of its namesake without all the consequences.

**14 muffins**

Filling

- 5 tablespoons finely ground almonds
- 1/4 cup plain dry bread crumbs
- 1 tablespoon brown sugar
- 1/8 teaspoon salt
- 2 tablespoons plus 2 teaspoons honey
- 2 teaspoons water
- 1 teaspoon almond extract
- 1 tablespoon light butter, room temperature

Streusel topping

- 1/4 cup granulated sugar
- 1/4 cup all-purpose flour
- 1 1/2 tablespoons light butter, room temperature

Batter

- 2 cups all-purpose flour
- 1/2 cup whole wheat flour
- 3/4 cup granulated sugar
- 3/4 teaspoon salt
- 1 tablespoon baking powder
- 1/2 teaspoon ground cinnamon
- 3/4 cup 2 percent milk
- 1/2 cup lowfat buttermilk
- 1/3 cup lowfat ricotta cheese
- 2 large egg whites
- 1 tablespoon canola oil
- 1 tablespoon vanilla extract
- 1 tablespoon butter-flavored extract

Icing

- 1 cup powdered sugar
- 1 tablespoon plus 1 teaspoon orange juice
- 1/2 teaspoon vanilla extract

Preheat oven to 375 degrees F. Line a muffin pan with paper muffin cups and lightly coat them with vegetable or canola oil spray.

Prepare filling: In a mixing bowl combine all ingredients, except the butter, and stir with a fork then add the butter and combine well. Set aside.

Prepare streusel: Combine all ingredients in a small mixing bowl and rub mixture together with your fingers to completely distribute the butter. Mixture will resemble coarse crumbs.

Prepare batter: In large mixing bowl combine both flours, sugar, salt, baking powder, and cinnamon. In a separate mixing bowl combine all remaining ingredients and whisk together until smooth. Pour into dry ingredients and mix just until all ingredients are moist.

Fill prepared muffin cups halfway and put a heaping teaspoon of the filling in the center of each one. Press the filling down into the batter slightly. Cover with the remaining batter, filling to the rims, and sprinkle the top of each muffin with some of the streusel topping. Bake for approximately 20 minutes. Muffins should be light golden brown, and a cake tester inserted just off to the side of the filling should come out clean.

Cool in pan for 10 minutes before removing to cool completely.

Prepare icing: In a small bowl combine all ingredients and stir until smooth. Drizzle some of the icing over each muffin, using a spoon. Icing should flow easily from the spoon. You may thin it with a little more orange juice if you need a thinner consistency.

Store in an airtight container.

## Hint

Because this is supposed to be a lower fat recipe, I kept the fat-filled ingredients to a minimum. But counterfeiting the famous bear claw pastry is no easy task when you're avoiding fat! If you can't resist, go ahead and sprinkle some sliced almonds over the top of the glaze before it sets for that authentic bear claw look!

### Each Serving Provides

255 Calories, 17% from Fat, 5 g Fat, 48 g Carbohydrates, 6 g Protein, 84 mg Calcium, 2 g Dietary Fiber, 259 mg Sodium, 7 mg Cholesterol.

# Anisette Muffins

Every year when I was growing up, my mother would make
these wonderful German Christmas cookies that were flavored
with anise, which tastes like black licorice, only milder, when
you bake with it. They are to this day one of my favorite cookies.
So I decided to make an anisette muffin. If you like the
flavor of anise, you'll love these muffins.

**14 muffins**

| | | | |
|---|---|---|---|
| 2½ | cups all-purpose flour | ¼ | cup canola oil |
| 1 | cup granulated sugar | ½ | cup lowfat ricotta cheese |
| ½ | teaspoon salt | 2 | large egg whites |
| 1 | tablespoon baking powder | 2 | teaspoons vanilla extract |
| 1 | teaspoon baking soda | 1 | tablespoon anise extract |
| ½ | cup lowfat buttermilk | ⅓ | to ½ cup powdered sugar |
| ¾ | cup 2 percent milk | | to dust muffin tops |

Preheat oven to 375 degrees F. Line a muffin pan with paper muffin cups and lightly coat them with vegetable or canola oil spray.

In a large mixing bowl combine flour, sugar, salt, baking powder, and baking soda. In a separate mixing bowl combine all remaining ingredients except powdered sugar, and whisk together until smooth. Pour into dry ingredients and mix just until all ingredients are moist.

Spoon batter into prepared muffin cups, filling to the rims, and dust the tops with powdered sugar using a fine mesh sieve. Bake for approximately 20 minutes. Muffins should be light golden brown, and a cake tester inserted into the center should come out clean.

Cool in pan for 10 minutes before removing to cool completely. You may want to give muffins an additional dusting of sugar once they have cooled. Store in an airtight container.

### Each Serving Provides

209 Calories, 23% from Fat, 5 g Fat, 35 g Carbohydrates, 5 g Protein,
87 mg Calcium, 1 g Dietary Fiber, 254 mg Sodium, 5 mg Cholesterol.

# Raisin Bran Muffins

These are delicious when served warm with a pat of light butter
or even a small dollop of your favorite jam or jelly.

**18 muffins**

| | |
|---|---|
| 2 cups all-purpose flour | 1/2 cup lowfat ricotta cheese |
| 1 1/2 cups wheat bran | 1/2 cup 2 percent milk |
| 3/4 cup granulated sugar | 2 tablespoons molasses |
| 1 tablespoon baking powder | 2 tablespoons honey |
| 1 teaspoon baking soda | 1 whole large egg plus 2 egg |
| 1/2 teaspoon salt | whites |
| 1 cup raisins or sultanas | 2 tablespoons canola oil |
| 2/3 cup lowfat buttermilk | 1 tablespoon vanilla extract |

Preheat oven to 375 degrees F. Line a muffin pan with paper muffin cups and lightly coat them with vegetable or canola oil spray.

In a large mixing bowl combine flour, bran, sugar, baking powder, baking soda, salt, and raisins. In a separate mixing bowl combine all remaining ingredients and whisk together until smooth. Pour into dry ingredients and mix just until all ingredients are moist.

Spoon batter into prepared muffin cups, filling to the rims, and bake for approximately 20 minutes. Muffins should be light golden brown, and a cake tester inserted into the center should come out clean.

Cool muffins in pan for 10 minutes before removing to cool completely. Store in an airtight container.

### Each Serving Provides

170 Calories, 16% from Fat, 3 g Fat, 33 g Carbohydrates, 5 g Protein,
79 mg Calcium, 3 g Dietary Fiber, 215 mg Sodium, 16 mg Cholesterol.

Muffins with Coffee Cake Appeal

# Sesame and Honey Almond Muffins

This recipe is for those of you who feel like being adventurous.
East meets West in the unique flavor of these muffins.
They're delicious for breakfast, but don't stop there:
try them with Asian or Thai food!

**15 muffins**

2 1/2 cups all-purpose flour
1/4 cup granulated sugar
1/4 cup brown sugar, firmly
packed
1/2 teaspoon salt
1 tablespoon baking powder
1 teaspoon baking soda
1/3 cup finely ground toasted
almonds
1/2 cup honey
1/2 cup lowfat buttermilk

3/4 cup 2 percent milk
2 tablespoons sesame oil
1/3 cup lowfat ricotta cheese
1 large whole egg plus 1 egg
white
1 tablespoon vanilla extract
1 teaspoon almond extract
3 tablespoons sesame seeds
for muffin tops

Preheat oven to 375 degrees F. Line a muffin pan with paper muffin cups and lightly coat them with vegetable or canola oil spray.

In a large mixing bowl combine flour, both sugars, salt, baking powder, baking soda, and ground almonds. In a separate mixing bowl combine all remaining ingredients except the sesame seeds, and whisk together until smooth. Pour into dry ingredients and mix just until all ingredients are moist.

Spoon batter into prepared muffin cups, filling to the rims, and sprinkle the top of each muffin with 1/2 teaspoon of the sesame seeds. Bake for approximately 20 minutes. Muffins should be light golden brown and a cake tester inserted into the center should come out clean.

Cool muffins in pan for 10 minutes before removing to cool completely. Store in an airtight container.

## Each Serving Provides

209 Calories, 24% from Fat, 6 g Fat, 35 g Carbohydrates, 5 g Protein,
97 mg Calcium, 1 g Dietary Fiber, 244 mg Sodium, 18 mg Cholesterol.

# Five-Grain Muffins

Grains are the hot ticket these days when it comes to a healthy diet. However, making them taste delicious is another story! This combination of different grains along with sweet brown sugar makes for a deliciously healthy muffin.

### 15 muffins

1 1/4 cups all-purpose flour
3/4 cup whole wheat flour
1/3 cup barley flour
1/3 cup oat bran
1/3 cup wheat bran
1 cup brown sugar, firmly packed
3/4 teaspoon salt
1 tablespoon baking powder

1 teaspoon baking soda
3/4 cup lowfat buttermilk
3/4 cup 2 percent milk
1/3 cup lowfat ricotta cheese
1 large egg plus 1 large egg white
2 tablespoons canola oil
1 tablespoon vanilla extract

Preheat oven to 375 degrees F. Line a muffin pan with paper muffin cups and lightly coat them with vegetable or canola oil spray.

In a large mixing bowl combine all the flours and brans, sugar, salt, baking powder, and baking soda. In a separate mixing bowl combine all remaining ingredients and whisk together until smooth. Pour into dry ingredients and mix just until all ingredients are moist.

Spoon into prepared muffin cups, filling to the rims, and bake for approximately 20 minutes. Muffins should be light golden brown and a cake tester inserted into the center should come out clean.

Cool muffins in pan for 10 minutes before removing to cool completely. Store in an airtight container.

## Hint

These muffins are delicious when you add 1/2 cup chopped raisins or sultanas. You can also try other types of flours in place of the ones called for if you want to experiment a bit. Just keep the proportions the same.

### Each Serving Provides

178 Calories, 18% from Fat, 4 g Fat, 33 g Carbohydrates, 5 g Protein, 90 mg Calcium, 2 g Dietary Fiber, 289 mg Sodium, 19 mg Cholesterol.

# Fruity Muffins

# Banana Muffins

If you love banana bread you're going to love these muffins.
They're just as delicious with the option of adding
ground pecans for extra flavor and texture.

**15 muffins**

2½ cups all-purpose flour
½ cup granulated sugar
½ cup brown sugar, firmly
   packed
1 teaspoon salt
1 tablespoon baking powder
1 teaspoon baking soda
2 teaspoons ground allspice
⅓ cup lowfat buttermilk

1½ medium-sized bananas,
   very ripe
⅓ cup 2 percent milk
⅓ cup lowfat ricotta cheese
1 large whole egg plus 1 egg
   white
2 tablespoons canola oil
1 tablespoon vanilla extract

Preheat oven to 375 degrees F. Line a muffin pan with paper muffin cups and lightly coat them with vegetable or canola oil spray.

In a large mixing bowl combine flour, both sugars, salt, baking powder, baking soda, and allspice. In a food processor combine buttermilk and bananas, and puree until smooth. Transfer to a mixing bowl, add all other remaining ingredients, and whisk together until smooth. Pour into dry ingredients and mix just until all ingredients are moist.

Spoon batter into prepared muffin cups, filling to the rims, and bake for approximately 20 minutes. Muffins should be light golden brown and a cake tester inserted into the center should come out clean.

Cool muffins in pan for 10 minutes before removing to cool completely. Store in an airtight container.

## Variation
For Banana Nut Muffins add 3 tablespoons finely ground pecans to the dry ingredients.

### Each Serving Provides
180 Calories, 15% from Fat, 3 g Fat, 34 g Carbohydrates, 4 g Protein,
66 mg Calcium, 1 g Dietary Fiber, 310 mg Sodium, 18 mg Cholesterol.

Fruity Muffins

# Pear Walnut Muffins

Dried pears give these muffins an intense flavor
and a luscious, moist texture.

**16 muffins**

6 dried pear halves (8 if pears
are smaller in size)
1 cup water
2 tablespoons granulated
sugar
2½ cups all-purpose flour
¾ cup granulated sugar
½ teaspoon salt
1 tablespoon baking powder
1 teaspoon baking soda
1 teaspoon each:
ground cinnamon
ground allspice
ground ginger

½ cup finely ground walnuts
⅓ cup lowfat buttermilk
1 cup plus 2 tablespoons 2
percent milk
2 tablespoons canola oil
⅓ cup lowfat ricotta cheese
2 large egg whites
1 tablespoon vanilla extract
5½ tablespoons granulated
sugar for tops of muffins

Preheat oven to 375 degrees F. Line a muffin pan with paper muffin cups and lightly coat them with vegetable or canola oil spray.

Chop the pears into ½-inch pieces, removing any hard parts of the core. In a small saucepan combine chopped pears, water, and 2 tablespoons sugar. Simmer over medium-high heat for approximately 15 minutes, or until pears are tender. Remove from heat and set aside to cool.

When pears have cooled, puree them with any remaining liquid in a food processor until smooth. Set aside.

In a large mixing bowl combine flour, ¾ cup sugar, salt, baking powder, baking soda, spices, and walnuts. In a separate mixing bowl combine remaining ingredients except sugar, and whisk together until smooth. Whisk in the pear puree. Pour into dry ingredients and mix just until all ingredients are moist.

Spoon batter into prepared muffin cups, filling to the rims, and sprinkle the top of each muffin with a teaspoon of the remaining sugar. Bake for approximately 20 minutes. Muffins should be light golden brown, and a cake tester inserted into the center should come out clean.

Cool muffins in pan for 10 minutes before removing to cool completely. Store in an airtight container.

### Each Serving Provides

212 Calories, 23% from Fat, 5 g Fat, 37 g Carbohydrates, 5 g Protein, 75 mg Calcium, 1 g Dietary Fiber, 222 mg Sodium, 3 mg Cholesterol.

# Fresh Cranberry Muffins

When cranberries are in season, be sure to buy a few extra bags for the freezer so you can make these muffins whenever you like! These are far too good to have only at a certain time of the year.

**15 muffins**

1½ cups fresh cranberries (or thawed frozen)
3 tablespoons granulated sugar
2½ cups all-purpose flour
1 cup granulated sugar
½ teaspoon salt
1 tablespoon baking powder
1 teaspoon baking soda
½ cup lowfat buttermilk

¾ cup 2 percent milk
3 tablespoons canola oil
⅓ cup lowfat ricotta cheese
1 large whole egg plus 2 egg whites
1 tablespoon vanilla extract
1 tablespoon grated orange peel
6 tablespoons granulated sugar for tops of muffins

Preheat oven to 375 degrees F. Line a muffin pan with paper muffin cups and lightly coat them with vegetable or canola oil spray.

Put cranberries in a food processor and process until they are coarsely chopped. Transfer chopped cranberries to a bowl and toss with the 3 tablespoons of sugar. Set aside. In a large mixing bowl combine flour, 1 cup sugar, salt, baking powder, and baking soda. In a separate mixing bowl combine remaining ingredients except for sugar, and whisk together until smooth. Toss the chopped cranberries in the flour mixture until combined (this coats them and keeps the batter from turning too pink). Then pour in the liquid and mix just until all ingredients are moist.

Spoon batter into prepared muffin cups, filling to the rims, and sprinkle the top of each muffin with a teaspoon of the remaining sugar. Bake for approximately 20 minutes. Muffins should be light golden brown, and a cake tester inserted into the center should come out clean.

Cool muffins in pan for 10 minutes before removing to cool completely. Store in an airtight container.

## Variation

For Cranberry Blueberry Muffins reduce the amount of cranberries to 1 cup before chopping, and add ¾ cup blueberries before final mixing stage.

### Each Serving Provides

210 Calories, 18% from Fat, 4 g Fat, 39 g Carbohydrates, 5 g Protein, 70 mg Calcium, 1 g Dietary Fiber, 244 mg Sodium, 18 mg Cholesterol.

---

# Lemon Grapefruit Poppy-Seed Muffins

I admit, I get tired of the same old lemon and poppy-seed combination. There are so many other flavors that combine well with poppy seeds, why not enjoy some more of them? Adding some grapefruit gives this standard duo a refreshing lift. The subtle taste of the grapefruit really sets them off!

**12 muffins**

2 1/2 cups all-purpose flour
1 cup granulated sugar
3/4 teaspoon salt
1 tablespoon baking powder
1 1/2 tablespoons poppy seeds
1/2 cup lowfat buttermilk
1/3 cup 2 percent milk
2 tablespoons canola oil
1/3 cup lowfat ricotta
1 large whole egg plus 1 egg white

2 teaspoons vanilla extract
2 tablespoons fresh lemon juice
1/4 cup fresh grapefruit juice
1 tablespoon grated lemon peel
1 tablespoon grated grapefruit peel
1/4 cup granulated sugar to dust tops of muffins

Preheat oven to 375 degrees F. Line a muffin pan with paper muffin cups and lightly coat them with vegetable or canola oil spray.

In a large mixing bowl combine flour, 1 cup sugar, salt, baking powder, and poppy seeds. In a separate mixing bowl combine all remaining ingredients except for sugar, and whisk together until smooth. Pour into dry ingredients and mix just until all ingredients are moist.

Spoon batter into prepared muffin cups, filling to the rims, and sprinkle the top of each muffin with a teaspoon of the remaining sugar. Bake for approximately 20 minutes. Muffins should be light golden brown, and a cake tester inserted into the center should come out clean.

Cool muffins in pan for 10 minutes before removing to cool completely. Store in an airtight container.

## Each Serving Provides

228 Calories, 17% from Fat, 4 g Fat, 42 g Carbohydrates, 5 g Protein, 93 mg Calcium, 1 g Dietary Fiber, 244 mg Sodium, 21 mg Cholesterol.

# Zucchini Muffins

These muffins can't help but be moist as well as delicious. The addition of fresh grated zucchini is the magic here. This recipe is perfect to use at that time of year when every gardener I know is giving away zucchini—just be sure to use the small ones. The overgrown gargantuan ones don't have the same flavor.

**14 muffins**

1 1/4 cups all-purpose flour
1 1/4 cups whole wheat flour
1/2 cup granulated sugar
1/2 cup brown sugar, firmly packed
1 teaspoon salt
1 tablespoon baking powder
1 teaspoon baking soda
1 teaspoon each:
ground cinnamon
ground allspice
ground cloves

1/3 cup lowfat buttermilk
1/2 cup 2 percent milk
1/3 cup lowfat ricotta cheese
1 large whole egg plus 1 egg white
3 tablespoons canola oil
1 tablespoon vanilla extract
1 1/4 cups grated zucchini

Preheat oven to 375 degrees F. Line a muffin pan with paper muffin cups and lightly coat them with vegetable or canola oil spray.

In a large mixing bowl combine both flours, both sugars, salt, baking powder, baking soda, and spices. In a separate mixing bowl combine all remaining ingredients and whisk together until smooth. Pour into dry ingredients and mix just until all ingredients are moist. This will be a somewhat stiff batter because the zucchini releases moisture as it cooks.

Spoon batter into prepared muffin cups, filling to the rims, and bake for approximately 20 minutes. Muffins should be light golden brown, and a cake tester inserted into the center should come out clean.

Cool muffins in pan for 10 minutes before removing to cool completely. Store in an airtight container.

## Each Serving Provides

192 Calories, 21% from Fat, 4 g Fat, 34 g Carbohydrates, 5 g Protein, 82 mg Calcium, 2 g Dietary Fiber, 327 mg Sodium, 18 mg Cholesterol.

# Pumpkin Spice Muffins

No need to wait for the holidays to taste the flavor of pumpkin pie, you can have one of these instead! You can enjoy these year-round, but they're also great for Halloween parties or even on the Thanksgiving table—just tell the pie to move on over!

**12 muffins**

| | |
|---|---|
| 2½ cups all-purpose flour | ⅓ cup lowfat buttermilk |
| ½ cup granulated sugar | ½ cup 2 percent milk |
| ½ cup brown sugar, firmly packed | 2 tablespoons canola oil |
| ½ teaspoon salt | ⅓ cup lowfat ricotta cheese |
| 1 tablespoon baking powder | 1 large whole egg plus 1 egg white |
| 1 teaspoon baking soda | 1 tablespoon vanilla extract |
| 1 teaspoon each: ground nutmeg ground cinnamon ground ginger | ½ cup plus 2 tablespoons canned pumpkin |

Preheat oven to 375 degrees F. Line a muffin pan with paper muffin cups and lightly coat them with vegetable or canola oil spray.

In a large mixing bowl combine flour, both sugars, salt, baking powder, baking soda, and spices. In a separate mixing bowl combine all remaining ingredients and whisk together until smooth. Pour into dry ingredients and mix just until all ingredients are moist.

Spoon batter into prepared muffin cups, filling to the rims, and bake for approximately 20 minutes. Muffins should be light golden brown, and a cake tester inserted into the center should come out clean.

Cool muffins in pan for 10 minutes before removing to cool completely. Store in an airtight container.

### Each Serving Provides

219 Calories, 16% from Fat, 4 g Fat, 40 g Carbohydrates, 5 g Protein, 90 mg Calcium, 1 g Dietary Fiber, 293 mg Sodium, 21 mg Cholesterol.

# Blueberry Muffins

Bursting with blueberries, here is a lowfat
rendition of a classic muffin.

**16 muffins**

2 1/2 cups all-purpose flour
1 cup granulated sugar
1/2 teaspoon salt
1 tablespoon baking powder
1 teaspoon baking soda
1/2 cup lowfat buttermilk
3/4 cup 2 percent milk
2 tablespoons canola oil

1/3 cup lowfat ricotta cheese
1 large whole egg plus 2 egg whites
1 tablespoon vanilla extract
1 tablespoon grated lemon peel
1 1/3 cups fresh or frozen blueberries

Preheat oven to 375 degrees F. Line a muffin pan with paper muffin cups and lightly coat them with vegetable or canola oil spray.

In a large mixing bowl combine flour, sugar, salt, baking powder, and baking soda. In a separate mixing bowl combine all remaining ingredients except for blueberries, and whisk together until smooth. Toss the blueberries in the flour mixture and then pour in the wet ingredients. Mix just until all ingredients are moist.

Spoon batter into prepared muffin cups, filling to the rims, and bake for approximately 20 minutes. Muffins should be light golden brown, and a cake tester inserted into the center should come out clean.

Cool muffins in pan for 10 minutes before removing to cool completely. Store in an airtight container.

## Variation

Blueberry Streusel Muffins. In a small mixing bowl combine 1/3 cup granulated sugar, 3 tablespoons all-purpose flour, and 1 1/2 tablespoons softened light butter. Rub mixture together with your fingers to make coarse crumbs and top each muffin with some of the streusel before baking them.

### Each Serving Provides

167 Calories, 17% from Fat, 3 g Fat, 30 g Carbohydrates, 4 g Protein,
66 mg Calcium, 1 g Dietary Fiber, 225 mg Sodium, 16 mg Cholesterol.

# Raspberry and Ginger Streusel Muffins

The addition of ground ginger to the streusel topping is what makes these muffins taste so unusually delicious.

**16 muffins**

Streusel topping
- ½ cup granulated sugar
- ¼ cup all-purpose flour
- 2 teaspoons ground ginger
- 2 tablespoons light butter, room temperature

Batter
- 2½ cups all-purpose flour
- 1 cup granulated sugar
- ½ teaspoon salt
- 1 tablespoon baking powder
- 1 teaspoon baking soda
- 1 teaspoon baking soda
- ½ cup lowfat buttermilk
- ¾ cup 2 percent milk
- 2 tablespoons canola oil
- ⅓ cup lowfat ricotta cheese
- 1 large whole egg plus 2 egg whites
- 1 tablespoon vanilla extract
- 1 tablespoon grated lemon peel
- 1½ cups whole raspberries, fresh or unsweetened frozen

Preheat oven to 375 degrees F. Line a muffin pan with paper muffin cups and lightly coat them with vegetable or canola oil spray.

Prepare streusel: In a small mixing bowl combine all ingredients. Rub mixture together with your fingers to make coarse crumbs and set aside.

Prepare batter: In a large mixing bowl combine flour, sugar, salt, baking powder, and baking soda. In a separate mixing bowl combine all remaining ingredients except for raspberries, and whisk together until smooth. Toss the raspberries in the flour mixture (this coats them and keeps the batter from turning too pink). Then pour in the liquid mixture and mix just until all ingredients are moist.

Spoon batter into prepared muffin cups, filling to the rims, and top each muffin with some of the streusel topping. Bake for approximately 20 minutes. Muffins should be light golden brown, and a cake tester inserted into the center should come out clean.

Cool muffins in pan for 10 minutes before removing to cool completely. Store in an airtight container.

### Each Serving Provides

204 Calories, 17% from Fat, 4 g Fat, 38 g Carbohydrates, 5 g Protein, 68 mg Calcium, 1 g Dietary Fiber, 234 mg Sodium, 19 mg Cholesterol.

Fruity Muffins

# Carrot Raisin Muffins

No muffin book would be complete without this old favorite.
If you are fond of carrot cake, you will be equally
fond of these muffins.

**16 muffins**

| | |
|---|---|
| 2 cups all-purpose flour | $\frac{1}{2}$ cup raisins or sultanas, |
| $\frac{1}{2}$ cup whole wheat flour | chopped |
| $\frac{1}{2}$ cup granulated sugar | $\frac{1}{2}$ cup 2 percent milk |
| $\frac{1}{2}$ cup brown sugar, firmly | $\frac{1}{3}$ cup lowfat ricotta cheese |
| packed | $\frac{1}{2}$ cup orange juice |
| 1 teaspoon salt | 1 large egg plus 1 large egg |
| 1 tablespoon baking powder | white |
| 1 teaspoon baking soda | $\frac{1}{4}$ cup canola oil |
| 1 teaspoon ground allspice | 1 tablespoon vanilla extract |
| 1 teaspoon ground cinnamon | $1\frac{1}{4}$ cups grated carrots (washed |
| $\frac{1}{2}$ teaspoon ground cloves | and peeled) |
| $\frac{1}{2}$ teaspoon ground ginger | |

Preheat oven to 375 degrees F. Line a muffin pan with paper muffin cups and lightly coat them with vegetable or canola oil spray.

In a large mixing bowl combine both flours, brown sugar, granulated sugar, salt, baking powder, baking soda, spices, and raisins. In a separate mixing bowl combine all remaining ingredients except carrots, and whisk together until smooth. Stir in the grated carrots. Pour into dry ingredients and mix just until all ingredients are moist.

Spoon into prepared muffin cups, filling to the rims, and bake for approximately 20 to 25 minutes. Muffins should be light golden brown, and a cake tester inserted into the center should come out clean.

Cool muffins in pan for 10 minutes before removing to cool completely. Store in an airtight container.

## Variation

Try adding ½ cup grated parsnips in place of ½ cup of carrots for a delicious change. Small parsnips are best because they are the most tender. The core of larger parsnips has a woody and fibrous texture. If you must use larger ones, be sure to remove and discard the core before grating them.

### Each Serving Provides

193 Calories, 22% from Fat, 5 g Fat, 34 g Carbohydrates, 4 g Protein, 65 mg Calcium, 2 g Dietary Fiber, 284 mg Sodium, 15 mg Cholesterol.

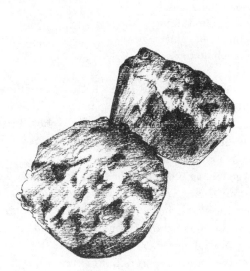

Fruity Muffins

# Sugar Plum Muffins

When I was a child, my grandmother would often tell me the story
of the sugar plum tree, from a poem by Eugene Field, at bedtime,
with the hopes of getting me to fall asleep. To this day the
story stays with me, as does my fondness for fresh plums.
This was my inspiration for the sugar plum muffin.

**16 muffins**

2 medium-sized firm, ripe
   plums
2½ cups all-purpose flour
1 cup granulated sugar
1 teaspoon salt
1 tablespoon baking powder
1 teaspoon baking soda
1 teaspoon ground allspice
½ teaspoon ground ginger
½ cup lowfat buttermilk

¾ cup 2 percent milk
¼ cup lowfat ricotta cheese
1 large egg plus 2 large egg
   whites
2 tablespoons canola oil
1 tablespoon grated orange
   peel
1 tablespoon vanilla extract
5½ tablespoons granulated
   sugar for tops of muffins

Preheat oven to 375 degrees F. Line a muffin pan with paper muffin cups and lightly coat them with vegetable or canola oil spray.

Quarter the plums, removing the pits, and chop them in a food
processor until they are coarse, but not pureed. You should have
approximately 1 cup of chopped plums.

In a large mixing bowl combine flour, 1 cup sugar, salt, baking
powder, baking soda, and spices. In a separate mixing bowl combine all remaining ingredients except for sugar, and whisk together
until smooth. Stir in the chopped plums. Pour into dry ingredients
and mix just until all ingredients are moist.

Spoon batter into prepared muffin cups, filling to the rims,
and top each muffin with a teaspoon of the remaining sugar. Bake
for approximately 20 minutes.

Muffins should be light golden brown, and a cake tester inserted into the center should come out clean.

Cool muffins in pan for 10 minutes before removing to cool
completely. Store in an airtight container.

Each Serving Provides

179 Calories, 15% from Fat, 3 g Fat, 34 g Carbohydrates, 4 g Protein,
60 mg Calcium, 1 g Dietary Fiber, 290 mg Sodium, 15 mg Cholesterol.

# Savory Muffins

# Parmesan and Fresh Herb Muffins

Muffins aren't just for the breakfast table anymore. Try serving these instead of the usual French bread the next time you have spaghetti or any other Italian food.

**14 muffins**

| | | | |
|---|---|---|---|
| 2½ | cups all-purpose flour | ¾ | cup lowfat buttermilk |
| ⅓ | cup whole wheat flour | ¾ | cup 2 percent milk |
| 1 | tablespoon baking powder | ⅓ | cup lowfat ricotta cheese |
| 1 | teaspoon baking soda | 1 | large whole egg plus 2 egg whites |
| 1¼ | teaspoons salt | | |
| ½ | teaspoon fresh ground pepper | 1 | tablespoon canola oil |
| ⅓ | cup finely grated Parmesan cheese | ½ | teaspoon minced fresh garlic |
| 2 | teaspoons each of chopped fresh herbs: parsley rosemary thyme oregano | | |

Preheat oven to 375 degrees F. Line a muffin pan with paper muffin cups and lightly coat them with vegetable or canola oil spray.

In a large mixing bowl combine both flours, baking powder, baking soda, salt, pepper, cheese, and herbs. In a separate mixing bowl combine all remaining ingredients and whisk together until smooth. Pour into dry ingredients and mix just until all ingredients are moist.

Spoon batter into prepared muffin cups, filling to the rims, and bake for approximately 20 minutes. Muffins should be light golden brown, and a cake tester inserted into the center should come out clean.

Cool muffins in pan for 10 minutes before removing to cool completely. Store in an airtight container.

### Each Serving Provides

136 Calories, 20% from Fat, 3 g Fat, 21 g Carbohydrates, 6 g Protein, 105 mg Calcium, 1 g Dietary Fiber, 409 mg Sodium, 20 mg Cholesterol.

Savory Muffins

# Sun-Dried Tomato and Rosemary Muffins

Among the other herbs in my garden, my rosemary bush definitely has seniority. Because it was the first planted, it has outgrown all the others. So, I love creating recipes to utilize this wonderfully fragrant herb. These muffins were inspired by my vine-ripened tomato-rosemary sauce. They are perfect with many Italian dishes.

**12 muffins**

| | |
|---|---|
| 2¾ cups all-purpose flour | ¾ cup 2 percent milk |
| 2 teaspoons salt | ⅓ cup lowfat ricotta cheese |
| ½ teaspoon fresh ground pepper | 1 large whole egg plus 2 egg whites |
| 1 tablespoon baking powder | 1 tablespoon canola oil |
| 1 teaspoon baking soda | ½ teaspoon minced fresh garlic |
| 1 tablespoon plus 1 teaspoon chopped fresh rosemary | ⅓ cup finely chopped sun-dried tomatoes, oil packed |
| ½ cup lowfat buttermilk | |

Preheat oven to 375 degrees F. Line a muffin pan with paper muffin cups and lightly coat them with vegetable or canola oil spray.

In a large mixing bowl combine flour, salt, pepper, baking powder, baking soda, and rosemary. In a separate mixing bowl combine all remaining ingredients and whisk together until smooth. Pour into dry ingredients and mix just until all ingredients are moist.

Spoon batter into prepared muffin cups, filling to the rims, and bake for approximately 20 minutes. Muffins should be light golden brown, and a cake tester inserted into the center should come out clean.

Cool muffins in pan for 10 minutes before removing to cool completely. Store in an airtight container.

## Hint

For an extra touch, sprinkle the tops of muffins with additional rosemary, unchopped, before baking them.

### Each Serving Provides

151 Calories, 18% from Fat, 3 g Fat, 25 g Carbohydrates, 6 g Protein, 88 mg Calcium, 1 g Dietary Fiber, 570 mg Sodium, 21 mg Cholesterol.

# Corn and Pepper Jack Cheese Muffins

The addition of whole corn kernels and grated pepper Jack cheese make these so much more exciting than the usual corn muffin. They are delicious served with chili or any other hot spicy Mexican or Southwestern style dish.

**14 muffins**

1 1/2 cups all-purpose flour
1 cup yellow cornmeal
1 teaspoon salt
1 tablespoon baking powder
1 teaspoon baking soda
2 tablespoons granulated sugar
3/4 cup grated pepper Jack cheese
1/2 cup lowfat buttermilk

3/4 cup 2 percent milk
1 large whole egg plus 1 egg white
1 tablespoon canola oil
1 tablespoon honey
1/4 teaspoon minced fresh garlic
1 1/2 cups cooked corn kernels, canned or fresh

Preheat oven to 375 degrees F. Line a muffin pan with paper muffin cups and lightly coat them with vegetable or canola oil spray.

In a large mixing bowl combine flour, cornmeal, salt, baking powder, baking soda, sugar, and cheese. In a separate mixing bowl combine all remaining ingredients and whisk together until smooth. Pour into dry ingredients and mix just until all ingredients are moist.

Spoon batter into prepared muffin cups, filling to the rims, and bake for approximately 20 minutes. Muffins should be light golden brown, and a cake tester inserted into the center should come out clean.

Cool muffins in pan for 10 minutes before removing to cool completely. Store in an airtight container.

### Each Serving Provides

159 Calories, 22% from Fat, 4 g Fat, 26 g Carbohydrates, 6 g Protein, 88 mg Calcium, 1 g Dietary Fiber, 357 mg Sodium, 21 mg Cholesterol.

Savory Muffins

# Parsley Potato Muffins

It's the addition of russet potatoes that make these muffins
so delicate and moist. They are like eating potato dumplings,
only in muffin form. These are a fantastic accompaniment
to stews or pot roast.

**15 muffins**

| | | | |
|---|---|---|---|
| 2 | small russet potatoes, approximately 3 inches long by 2 1/2 inches wide, peeled and cut into 1-inch chunks | 1 | teaspoon baking soda |
| | | 1/4 | cup chopped fresh parsley |
| | | 1/2 | cup lowfat buttermilk |
| | | 3/4 | cup 2 percent milk |
| 2 1/2 | cups all-purpose flour | 2 | tablespoons canola oil |
| 1 1/2 | teaspoons salt | 1 | large whole egg plus 1 egg white |
| 1/2 | teaspoon fresh ground pepper | 1/2 | teaspoon minced fresh garlic |
| 1 | tablespoon baking powder | | |

Preheat oven to 375 degrees F. Line a muffin pan with paper muffin cups and lightly coat them with vegetable or canola oil spray.

Place the potatoes in a small saucepan and add enough water to cover them by an inch. Cook over medium-high heat until tender but not mushy. Drain potatoes, reserving 1/2 cup of the liquid, and set aside to cool.

In a large mixing bowl combine flour, salt, pepper, baking powder, baking soda, and parsley. In a food processor combine cooled potatoes, potato liquid, buttermilk, and 2 percent milk, and process until smooth. Transfer to a mixing bowl, add oil, eggs, and garlic, and whisk together until smooth. Pour into dry ingredients and mix just until all ingredients are moist.

Spoon batter into prepared muffin cups, filling to the rims, and bake for approximately 20 minutes. Muffins should be light golden brown, and a cake tester inserted into the center should come out clean.

Cool muffins in pan for 10 minutes before removing to cool completely. Store in an airtight container.

### Each Serving Provides

126 Calories, 19% from Fat, 3 g Fat, 21 g Carbohydrates, 4 g Protein,
43 mg Calcium, 1 g Dietary Fiber, 381 mg Sodium, 16 mg Cholesterol.

# Fresh Basil and White Bean Muffins

It's hard to turn down anything when it has aromatic fresh basil in it. These muffins are very hearty with tender white beans, extra virgin olive oil, and plenty of fresh chopped basil.

**16 muffins**

2 1/2 cups all-purpose flour
1 teaspoon salt
1/2 teaspoon fresh ground pepper
1 tablespoon baking powder
1 teaspoon baking soda
1/3 cup chopped fresh basil
1/2 cup lowfat buttermilk
3/4 cup 2 percent milk

1 large whole egg plus 1 egg white
3 tablespoons extra virgin olive oil
3/4 teaspoon minced fresh garlic
1 can (15 ounces) small white beans with liquid

Preheat oven to 375 degrees F. Line a muffin pan with paper muffin cups and lightly coat them with vegetable or canola oil spray.

In a large mixing bowl combine flour, salt, pepper, baking powder, baking soda, and basil. In a separate mixing bowl combine all remaining ingredients and whisk together until smooth. Pour into dry ingredients and mix just until all ingredients are moist.

Spoon batter into prepared muffin cups, filling to the rims, and bake for approximately 20 minutes. Muffins should be light golden brown, and a cake tester inserted into the center should come out clean.

Cool muffins in pan for 10 minutes before removing to cool completely. Store in an airtight container.

## Variations

Try adding 1/3 cup finely grated Parmesan cheese or chopped sun-dried tomatoes to this recipe for a real Italian taste!

### Each Serving Provides

147 Calories, 21% from Fat, 4 g Fat, 23 g Carbohydrates, 6 g Protein, 63 mg Calcium, 1 g Dietary Fiber, 161 mg Sodium, 14 mg Cholesterol.

Savory Muffins

# Roasted Red Pepper and Corn Muffins

I happen to love corn muffins any way I can get them, and these are one of my favorites! The addition of roasted red peppers makes these scrumptious. They're perfect with chili or stews.

**15 muffins**

| | | | |
|---|---|---|---|
| 2 | small red bell peppers | 1 | teaspoon baking soda |
| 2 | teaspoons olive oil | 3/4 | cup 2 percent milk |
| 1 1/2 | cups all-purpose flour | 1/2 | cup lowfat buttermilk |
| 1 | cup yellow cornmeal | 1 | large whole egg plus 1 egg white |
| 2 | tablespoons granulated sugar | | |
| 1 | teaspoon salt | 2 | tablespoons canola oil |
| 1 | tablespoon baking powder | 2 | tablespoons honey |

Preheat oven to 375 degrees F. Line a muffin pan with paper muffin cups and lightly coat them with vegetable or canola oil spray.

To roast peppers: You need either a gas or charcoal grill for the best results when roasting peppers. Get the grill very hot, then rub the outside of peppers with the olive oil. Place them on the grill and char the outsides evenly all the way around. When peppers are charred, place them in a bowl and cover with plastic wrap until they cool to room temperature. Use a small paring knife to scrape off the charred skins and discard them. Do not rinse the peppers under cold water as this washes away their precious oils.

Cut roasted peppers in half and remove seeds and membranes, then place in a food processor. Process peppers until they are roughly chopped, but not completely pureed. Set aside.

In a large mixing bowl combine flour, cornmeal, sugar, salt, baking powder, and baking soda. In a separate mixing bowl combine all remaining ingredients, including the peppers, and whisk together until smooth. Pour into dry ingredients and mix just until all ingredients are moist.

Spoon batter into prepared muffin cups, filling to the rims, and bake for approximately 20 minutes. Muffins should be light golden brown, and a cake tester inserted into the center should come out clean.

Cool muffins in pan for 10 minutes before removing to cool completely. Store in an airtight container.

### Each Serving Provides

136 Calories, 23% from Fat, 3 g Fat, 23 g Carbohydrates, 4 g Protein,
40 mg Calcium, 1 g Dietary Fiber, 310 mg Sodium, 16 mg Cholesterol.

# Russian Rye Muffins

I modeled these after one of my favorite breads. They are dark and dense with hints of chocolate, coffee, and molasses. Their subtly sweet flavor goes wonderfully with any kind of food.

## 12 muffins

1/4 cup strong black coffee
3 tablespoons molasses
3 tablespoons honey
1 ounce (1 square) unsweetened chocolate
1 cup all-purpose flour
1 cup whole wheat flour
1 cup dark rye flour
1 1/2 tablespoons baking powder
1 teaspoon salt

1/4 teaspoon ground cinnamon
1/4 teaspoon ground allspice
2 tablespoons granulated sugar
1/2 cup lowfat buttermilk
1/4 cup 2 percent milk
1 large whole egg plus 2 egg whites
1/3 cup lowfat ricotta cheese
3 tablespoons canola oil

Preheat oven to 375 degrees F. Line a muffin pan with paper muffin cups and lightly coat them with vegetable or canola oil spray.

In a small saucepan combine coffee, molasses, honey, and chocolate, and melt over low heat, stirring occasionally, until smooth. Set aside to cool.

In a large mixing bowl combine all the flours, baking powder, salt, spices, and sugar. In a separate mixing bowl combine all remaining ingredients, including the cooled chocolate mixture, and whisk together until smooth. Pour into dry ingredients and mix just until all ingredients are moist.

Spoon batter into prepared muffin cups, filling to the rims, and bake for approximately 20 minutes. A cake tester inserted into the center should come out clean (a few moist crumbs are OK).

Cool muffins in pan for 10 minutes before removing to cool completely. Store in an airtight container.

### Each Serving Provides

200 Calories, 28% from Fat, 6 g Fat, 33 g Carbohydrates, 6 g Protein, 93 mg Calcium, 3 g Dietary Fiber, 329 mg Sodium, 8 mg Cholesterol.

# Southwestern Black Bean Muffins

Loaded with black beans, cumin, fresh cilantro, and other spicy Southwest flavors, out of all the savory muffins, these are my husband's favorite. Once you try them, they may become yours as well!

**15 muffins**

| | | | |
|---|---|---|---|
| 2 1/2 | cups all-purpose flour | 2 | tablespoons canola oil |
| 1 1/2 | teaspoon salt | 1 | teaspoon minced garlic |
| 1/2 | teaspoon fresh ground pepper | 1 | tablespoon Tabasco jalapeño sauce |
| 1 | tablespoon baking powder | 1 1/2 | tablespoons chopped fresh cilantro |
| 1 | teaspoon baking soda | | |
| 1 1/2 | teaspoons ground cumin | 1 1/2 | cups cooked black beans (rinse and drain canned beans in a sieve with cold water) |
| 1 | teaspoon mild chili powder | | |
| 3/4 | cup 2 percent milk | | |
| 1/3 | cup lowfat ricotta cheese | | |
| 1 | large whole egg plus 2 egg whites | | |

Preheat oven to 375 degrees F. Line a muffin pan with paper muffin cups and lightly coat them with vegetable or canola oil spray.

In a large mixing bowl combine flour, salt, pepper, baking powder, baking soda, cumin, and chili powder. In a separate mixing bowl combine all remaining ingredients except for beans, and whisk together until smooth. Stir in black beans and pour into dry ingredients. Mix just until all ingredients are moist.

Spoon batter into prepared muffin cups, filling to the rims, and bake for approximately 20 minutes. Muffins should be light golden brown, and a cake tester inserted into the center should come out clean.

Cool muffins in pan for 10 minutes before removing to cool completely. Store in an airtight container.

## Hint

Want to turn up the heat on these babies? Try adding a little bit of finely minced jalapeño, or maybe a dash of habanero pepper sauce.

### Each Serving Provides

141 Calories, 21% from Fat, 3 g Fat, 22 g Carbohydrates, 6 g Protein,
69 mg Calcium, 1 g Dietary Fiber, 396 mg Sodium, 18 mg Cholesterol.

# Sour Cream and Caramelized Onion Muffins

Sour cream and onion are two tastes that are meant to go together, which gave me the idea for this muffin. Caramelizing the onions gives these muffins a rich and hearty flavor, perfectly complemented by the sour cream.

**14 muffins**

1 medium-sized onion, may be any variety you choose.
1 tablespoon extra virgin olive oil
pinch of salt and pepper
2½ cups all-purpose flour
1½ teaspoons salt
¼ teaspoon fresh ground pepper
1 tablespoon baking powder
1 teaspoon baking soda
½ cup lowfat buttermilk
¾ cup 2 percent milk
½ cup lowfat sour cream
1 large whole egg plus 2 egg whites
2 tablespoons extra virgin olive oil
½ teaspoon minced garlic

Preheat oven to 375 degrees F. Line a muffin pan with paper muffin cups and lightly coat them with vegetable or canola oil spray.

Peel the onion, cut it in half, and slice it thin. Put 1 tablespoon olive oil in a medium-sized sauté pan over high heat.

When the oil is hot, add the onions, tossing well. Sprinkle with salt and pepper and continue to cook the onions, stirring them often as they brown. If your burner is exceptionally hot, you may want to turn it down to medium high. Continue to cook the onions until they are caramelized to a golden brown, approximately 15 to 20 minutes. Set aside to cool. When onions are cool, chop them in a food processor and set aside.

In a large mixing bowl combine flour, salt, pepper, baking powder, and baking soda. In a separate mixing bowl combine all remaining ingredients, including the chopped onions, and whisk together until smooth. Pour into dry ingredients and mix just until all ingredients are moist.

Spoon batter into prepared muffin cups, filling to the rims, and bake for approximately 20 minutes. Muffins should be light golden brown, and a cake tester inserted into the center should come out clean.

Cool muffins in pan for 10 minutes before removing to cool completely. Store in an airtight container.

## Hint

These muffins are also delicious when you add ⅓ cup finely crumbled Gorgonzola cheese to the wet ingredients before mixing.

### Each Serving Provides

149 Calories, 29% from Fat, 5 g Fat, 22 g Carbohydrates, 5 g Protein,
59 mg Calcium, 1 g Dietary Fiber, 415 mg Sodium, 20 mg Cholesterol.

# Whole Wheat and
# Honey Mustard Muffins

The secret to these delicious muffins is the country-style
Dijon mustard that adds a subtle tang, which is
mellowed perfectly by the golden honey.

### 13 muffins

| | |
|---|---|
| 1½ cups all-purpose flour | 2 tablespoons canola oil |
| 1¼ cups whole wheat flour | 3 tablespoons honey |
| ¾ teaspoon salt | 1 large whole egg plus 2 egg |
| 1 tablespoon baking powder | whites |
| 1 teaspoon baking soda | 2 tablespoons country-style |
| ½ cup lowfat buttermilk | Dijon mustard |
| ¾ cup 2 percent milk | ½ teaspoon minced garlic |

Preheat oven to 375 degrees F. Line a muffin pan with paper muffin cups and lightly coat them with vegetable or canola oil spray.

In a large mixing bowl combine both flours, salt, baking powder, and baking soda. In a separate mixing bowl combine all remaining ingredients and whisk together until smooth. Pour into dry ingredients and mix just until all ingredients are moist.

Spoon batter into prepared muffin cups, filling to the rims, and bake for approximately 20 minutes. Muffins should be light golden brown, and a cake tester inserted into the center should come out clean.

Cool muffins in pan for 10 minutes before removing to cool completely. Store in an airtight container.

### Each Serving Provides

154 Calories, 21% from Fat, 4 g Fat, 26 g Carbohydrates, 5 g Protein,
53 mg Calcium, 2 g Dietary Fiber, 380 mg Sodium, 18 mg Cholesterol.

# PART TWO

# Other Heavenly Treats

For those days when you want something besides a muffin for breakfast—after all there are 365 mornings in the year to fill—you'll find plenty of delicious lowfat alternatives in the following chapters. Look for everything from piping hot scones and coffee cakes to fluffy pancakes and crisp waffles that will hold their own even on the weekend breakfast table. For added reward look to the chapter filled with dreamy syrups, fruity toppings, and heavenly flavored butters and spreads. These will serve as the perfect finishing touches to many of the goodies in this book.

# Scones

One of my fondest childhood memories is of the fresh, hot, raspberry-filled scones that we could only get at the state fair in Puyallup, Washington. Aside from all of the wild rides and farm animals that I looked forward to at the fair, I couldn't wait to get a bag of scones! They made them right there on the fairgrounds. There was always a long assembly line beginning with the person who mixed the dough, moving right down to the one who bagged them to be sold at the end of the line. And there was always a long line of people waiting for their scones to make the journey down that assembly line. The scones never had time to sit and cool because someone was there to snatch them up as soon as they were ready. They were always piping hot and oozing with raspberry jam.

Scones have made a real comeback. They are becoming increasingly popular as a choice for breakfast or an afternoon pick-me-up. You can find them now in most coffeehouses and bakeries, right alongside the muffins and other breakfast fare.

Like muffins, scones can be very high in fat and calories. The best ones I have ever had are made with real cream and lots of butter, so I don't have them very often! However, scones are still a wonderful treat even when they are made with less fat.

## Helpful Hints for Baking Perfect Scones

Scones are, in reality, just like biscuits and are made in much the same way. What makes the scone or biscuit so delicious? The texture! With the right ingredients and discipline in adhering to the best methods for mixing and baking, your scones will be flaky, moist, and irresistible. Here are some helping hints that pertain specifically to scone success.

## Scone Dough

Scones are mixed in much the same manner as a good pie crust. The butter or shortening is cut into the dry ingredients until only small particles of it are left suspended in the flour. Then the liquid is added and carefully mixed in so as not to overwork the dough and crush the particles of shortening. When the dough is baked, those small particles melt, leaving tiny pockets of air throughout the scone, creating the finished texture, which should be flaky and moist.

Obviously, the more shortening or butter, the better the scone. But for this book, I wanted to use as little fat as possible so I decided to use butter-flavored shortening instead. It has half the amount of saturated fat of butter, while still delivering a buttery flavor to the scone. It is also excellent for achieving a moist texture, even when only a small amount is used.

When mixing up the dough, it is a good idea to chill the shortening before cutting it into the dry ingredients. This will help those small fat particles retain their shape through the mixing process.

I prefer to mix the shortening into the dry ingredients with my hands. This allows better control and a more even distribution of the shortening. I simply rub the mixture together using my fingers until the shortening has been broken into very small particles.

When adding the liquid, use a fork to combine the ingredients just until they come together. Using a fork helps prevent overmixing, which results in a tough scone because the particles of shortening become completely worked into the dough.

## Cutting and Baking the Scones

### TRADITIONAL SCONES

First, turn the dough out on a lightly floured surface and knead it very slightly to form a ball. Then roll or pat it into a nine-inch circle. The dough will be very soft, so use the sharpest knife you can find to mark the circle into ten even wedges and cut them. It is helpful to wipe the knife after each cut if there is any dough stuck to it. If the dough is still sticking to the knife while you're cutting, lightly flour the blade between cuts.

Transfer the scones to a baking sheet, placing them at least one inch apart, and bake until light golden brown. Scones, like muffins, are baked for a short amount of time (approximately 20 minutes) at a high temperature (375 to 400 degrees Fahrenheit). The high temperature is necessary for them to rise and become golden. In the recipes that follow, I call for a specific temperature of 400 degrees, but you may have to adjust the temperature if your oven happens to run high or low by any significant amount.

### DROP SCONES

Lately I keep seeing drop scones in coffeehouses and bakeries everywhere. The ingredients are much the same as those of traditional scones, but the dough is dropped onto a cookie sheet instead of being rolled or cut. Drop scones are just as delicious as rolled scones and actually quicker to make, since you eliminate a few steps from the process.

Remember, there is nothing perfect about these babies. They are meant to look rustic and lumpy—that's part of their charm! Simply drop the dough onto the prepared cookie sheet as if you were making a giant drop cookie. Watch these closely while baking because they tend to bake a little faster than their rolled cousins, depending on your oven temperature. Their finished texture should be fluffy and tender inside, and crisp and light golden brown on the outside, but don't panic if they aren't brown enough—sometimes they have minds of their own!

## Storage

You should store your scones in airtight containers. The Tupperware type is best, but Ziploc bags work well, too.

# Whole Wheat and Honey Scones

The addition of whole wheat flour makes for a heartier textured scone. The whole wheat flavor is complemented perfectly by a brushing of golden honey over the top.

**10 scones**

| | |
|---|---|
| 1 cup all-purpose flour | 1/4 cup butter-flavored vege- |
| 1 cup whole wheat flour | table shortening, cold |
| 1/2 teaspoon salt | 3/4 cup lowfat buttermilk |
| 1 tablespoon plus 1 teaspoon | 1/4 cup honey |
| baking powder | 2 teaspoons vanilla extract |
| 1 tablespoon granulated | 1 to 2 tablespoons honey, to |
| sugar | brush over warm scones |

Preheat oven to 400 degrees F. Line a cookie sheet with foil or parchment paper.

In a large bowl combine both flours, salt, baking powder, and sugar. Add shortening and completely distribute by rubbing mixture together with your fingers. Mixture will be coarse. In a separate mixing bowl combine all remaining ingredients except honey, and whisk together until smooth. Pour into dry ingredients and mix with a fork to form a soft dough, being careful not to overwork.

Turn dough out onto a lightly floured surface and knead just enough to form a ball. Roll or pat dough into a 9-inch circle. Cut circle into 10 even wedges, using a sharp knife.

Place scones on prepared cookie sheet, at least 1 inch apart, and bake for 20 to 25 minutes or until scones are light golden brown.

Transfer scones to a rack and brush the tops with the remaining honey. Cool scones completely and store in an airtight container.

### Each Serving Provides

178 Calories, 27% from Fat, 5 g Fat, 29 g Carbohydrates, 4 g Protein, 37 mg Calcium, 2 g Dietary Fiber, 171 mg Sodium, 1 mg Cholesterol.

# Old-Fashioned Scones with Raspberry Jam

These are modeled after the delicious scones, piping hot and oozing with raspberry jam, that I always got as a child at the state fair in Puyallup, Washington. Be sure to serve them warm, or better yet, eat them right after they come out of the oven!

**10 scones**

| | |
|---|---|
| 2 cups all-purpose flour | ³/₄ cup lowfat buttermilk |
| ¹/₂ teaspoon salt | ¹/₄ cup lowfat ricotta cheese |
| 1 tablespoon plus 1 teaspoon baking powder | 1 tablespoon vanilla extract |
| 2 tablespoons granulated sugar | 1 egg white, beaten until frothy |
| ¹/₄ cup butter-flavored vegetable shortening, cold | 3 tablespoons granulated sugar |
| | ¹/₂ cup seedless raspberry jam |

Preheat oven to 400 degrees F. Line a cookie sheet with foil or parchment paper.

In a large mixing bowl combine flour, salt, baking powder, and 2 tablespoons sugar. Add shortening and completely distribute by rubbing mixture together with your fingers. Mixture will be coarse. In a separate mixing bowl combine buttermilk, ricotta, and vanilla, and whisk together until smooth. Pour into dry ingredients and mix with a fork to form a soft dough, being careful not to overwork the dough.

Turn dough out onto a lightly floured surface and knead just enough to form a ball. Roll or pat dough into a 9-inch circle. Brush top of circle with the beaten egg white and sprinkle with the remaining 3 tablespoons sugar. Cut circle into 10 even wedges, using a sharp knife.

Place wedges on prepared cookie sheet, at least 1 inch apart, and bake for 20 to 25 minutes or until scones are light golden brown.

Serve them warm from the oven, or cool on a rack. Split scones in half and spread each with 1 1/2 teaspoons of raspberry jam or store them in an airtight container to have later.

## Variations

These scones are wonderful when filled with any kind of jam or jelly that your heart desires, especially the homemade jam that comes from Grandma's house!

For Chocolate Chip Scones add 5 tablespoons mini chocolate chips to the dry ingredients.

### Each Serving Provides

224 Calories, 23% from Fat, 6 g Fat, 38 g Carbohydrates, 5 g Protein, 69 mg Calcium, 1 g Dietary Fiber, 181 mg Sodium, 3 mg Cholesterol.

Scones

# Banana Nut Scones

There's banana bread, so why shouldn't there be banana scones? Here's everything you love about banana bread and everything you love about scones all wrapped up in one delicious little package.

**10 Scones**

2 cups all-purpose flour
1 tablespoon plus 1 teaspoon baking powder
1/2 teaspoon salt
1/4 teaspoon each:
   ground cinnamon
   ground allspice
   ground cloves
1/4 cup plus 1 tablespoon granulated sugar

2 tablespoons finely ground almonds
1/4 cup butter-flavored vegetable shortening, cold
1/2 cup lowfat buttermilk
1/2 cup ripe, mashed banana (approx. 1 small banana)
1 tablespoon vanilla extract
1 egg white, beaten until frothy
2 tablespoons granulated sugar for tops of scones

Preheat oven to 400 degrees F. Line a cookie sheet with foil or parchment paper.

In a large mixing bowl combine flour, baking powder, salt, spices, 1/4 cup plus 1 tablespoon sugar, and almonds. Add shortening and completely distribute by rubbing mixture together with your fingers. Mixture will be coarse. In a food processor combine buttermilk, banana, and vanilla, and process until smooth. Pour into dry ingredients and mix with a fork to form a soft dough, being careful not to overwork dough.

Turn dough out onto a lightly floured surface and knead just enough to form a ball. Roll or pat dough into a 9-inch circle. Brush the top with the beaten egg white and sprinkle with the remaining 2 tablespoons sugar. Cut into 10 even wedges using a sharp knife.

Place scones on prepared cookie sheet at least 1 inch apart and bake for 20 to 25 minutes or until scones are light golden brown.

Cool scones completely on a rack and store in an airtight container.

### Each Serving Provides

196 Calories, 28% from Fat, 6 g Fat, 31 g Carbohydrates, 4 g Protein, 32 mg Calcium, 1 g Dietary Fiber, 168 mg Sodium, 0 mg Cholesterol.

# Lemon Lime Scones

The taste of citrus gives a refreshing flavor to these scones. I like to spread mine with orange marmalade for a triple citrus effect!

**10 scones**

| | |
|---|---|
| 2 cups all-purpose flour | 1 tablespoon fresh lime juice |
| ½ teaspoon salt | 1 tablespoon grated lemon peel |
| 1 tablespoon plus 1 teaspoon baking powder | 1 tablespoon grated lime peel |
| ¼ cup granulated sugar | 1 egg white, beaten until frothy |
| ¼ cup butter-flavored vegetable shortening, cold | 3 tablespoons granulated sugar for tops of scones |
| ¾ cup lowfat buttermilk | |
| ¼ cup lowfat ricotta | |
| 1 tablespoon fresh lemon juice | |

Preheat oven to 400 degrees F. Line a cookie sheet with foil or parchment paper.

In a large mixing bowl combine flour, salt, baking powder, and ¼ cup sugar. Add shortening and completely distribute by rubbing mixture together with your fingers. Mixture will be coarse. In a separate mixing bowl combine buttermilk, ricotta, citrus juices, and citrus peel, and whisk together until smooth. Pour into dry ingredients and mix with a fork to form a soft dough, being careful not to overwork the dough.

Turn dough out onto a lightly floured surface and knead just enough to form a ball. Roll or pat dough into a 9-inch circle. Brush the top with the beaten egg white and sprinkle with the remaining 3 tablespoons sugar. Cut into 10 even wedges using a sharp knife.

Place scones on prepared cookie sheet at least 1 inch apart and bake for 20 to 25 minutes or until scones are light golden brown.

Cool scones completely on a rack and store in an airtight container.

### Each Serving Provides

187 Calories, 28% from Fat, 6 g Fat, 29 g Carbohydrates, 5 g Protein, 68 mg Calcium, 1 g Dietary Fiber, 180 mg Sodium, 3 mg Cholesterol.

# Chocolate Hazelnut Scones

So rich with the flavors of chocolate and hazelnut,
you might opt to have these scones for dessert. They are
even better when filled with light whipped topping.

**10 scones**

| | |
|---|---|
| 2¼ cups all-purpose flour | ¾ cup lowfat buttermilk |
| ¼ cup unsweetened cocoa | ¼ cup lowfat ricotta cheese |
| ¾ teaspoon salt | 2 teaspoons vanilla extract |
| 1 tablespoon plus 1 teaspoon baking powder | 1 tablespoon hazelnut liqueur |
| 4 tablespoons granulated sugar | 1 egg white, beaten until frothy |
| 2 tablespoons finely ground, toasted hazelnuts | 3 tablespoons granulated sugar for tops of scones |
| ¼ cup butter-flavored vegetable shortening, cold | |

Preheat oven to 400 degrees F. Line a cookie sheet with foil or parchment paper.

In a large mixing bowl combine flour, cocoa, salt, baking powder, 4 tablespoons sugar, and hazelnuts. Add shortening and completely distributed by rubbing mixture together with your fingers. Mixture will be coarse. In a separate mixing bowl combine all other ingredients except for egg white and sugar, and whisk together until smooth. Pour into dry ingredients and mix with a fork to form a soft dough, being careful not to overwork dough.

Turn dough out onto a lightly floured surface and knead just enough to form a ball. Roll or pat dough into a 9-inch circle. Brush the top with the beaten egg white and sprinkle with the remaining sugar. Cut into 10 even wedges using a sharp knife.

Place scones on prepared cookie sheet at least 1 inch apart and bake for 20 to 25 minutes or until scones are light golden brown.

Cool scones completely on a rack and store in an airtight container.

### Each Serving Provides

222 Calories, 29% from Fat, 7 g Fat, 34 g Carbohydrates, 5 g Protein,
72 mg Calcium, 1 g Dietary Fiber, 233 mg Sodium, 3 mg Cholesterol.

# Russian Rye Scones

Here is a scone modeled after one of my favorite breads.
These are a little less dark and sweet than Russian black bread,
and they offer a delightful hint of chocolate and molasses.

**10 scones**

1 1/2 cups all-purpose flour
3/4 cup rye flour
1/2 teaspoon salt
1 tablespoon plus 1 teaspoon
   baking powder
2 teaspoons unsweetened
   cocoa
3 tablespoons granulated
   sugar

1/4 cup butter-flavored vegetable shortening, cold
3/4 cup lowfat buttermilk
1/4 cup lowfat ricotta cheese
1 tablespoon honey
2 teaspoons molasses
2 teaspoons vanilla extract

Preheat oven to 400 degrees F. Line a cookie sheet with foil or
parchment paper.

In a large mixing bowl combine both flours, salt, baking powder, cocoa, and sugar. Add the shortening and rub mixture together with your fingers to completely distribute. Mixture will be
coarse. In a separate mixing bowl combine all remaining ingredients and whisk together until smooth. Pour into dry ingredients
and mix with a fork to form a soft dough, being careful not to overwork dough.

Turn dough out onto a lightly floured surface and knead just
enough to form a ball. Roll or pat dough into a 9-inch circle. Cut
into 10 even wedges using a sharp knife. Place scones on prepared
cookie sheet at least 1 inch apart and bake for 15 to 20 minutes or
until scones are light golden brown.

Cool scones completely on a rack and store in an airtight
container.

## Each Serving Provides

186 Calories, 28% from Fat, 6 g Fat, 29 g Carbohydrates, 4 g Protein,
85 mg Calcium, 2 g Dietary Fiber, 265 mg Sodium, 3 mg Cholesterol.

# Golden Cornmeal Scones

I don't know of too many people who don't like corn muffins. There is something very comforting about them, especially when they are fresh and hot from the oven, drizzled with butter or honey. These scones will give you that very same feeling. They rely on masa, a very fine cornmeal, to deliver the taste of corn muffins with the texture of a scone. I do not recommend regular cornmeal as a substitute, because it is roughly milled and will not produce the right texture. Be sure to try them with your favorite jam or jelly!

**10 scones**

1½  cups all-purpose flour
½  cup masa
¾  teaspoon salt
1  tablespoon plus 1 teaspoon baking powder
4  tablespoons granulated sugar
¼  cup butter-flavored vegetable shortening, cold

½  cup lowfat buttermilk
¼  cup lowfat ricotta cheese
2  tablespoons honey
1  tablespoon vanilla extract
1  egg white, beaten until frothy
3  tablespoons granulated sugar for tops of scones

Preheat oven to 400 degrees F. Line a cookie sheet with foil or parchment paper.

In a large mixing bowl combine flour, masa, salt, baking powder, and 4 tablespoons sugar. Add the shortening and completely distribute by rubbing mixture together with your fingers. Mixture will be coarse.

In a separate mixing bowl combine buttermilk, ricotta, honey, and vanilla, and whisk together until smooth. Pour into dry ingredients and mix with a fork to form a soft dough, being careful not to overwork the dough.

Turn dough out onto a lightly floured surface and knead just enough to form a ball. Roll or pat dough into a 9-inch circle. Brush top of circle with the beaten egg white and sprinkle with the remaining sugar. Cut circle into 10 even wedges using a sharp knife. Place wedges on prepared cookie sheet, at least 1 inch apart, and bake for 20 to 25 minutes or until scones are light golden brown.

Cool scones completely on a rack and store in an airtight container.

### Each Serving Provides

188 Calories, 28% from Fat, 6 g Fat, 29 g Carbohydrates, 4 g Protein, 65 mg Calcium, 1 g Dietary Fiber, 226 mg Sodium, 3 mg Cholesterol.

Scones

# Oat Bran Scones

Try having these in place of a bran muffin. They aren't made with as much bran and are much lighter in taste and texture.

**10 scones**

| | |
|---|---|
| 1 ½ cups all-purpose flour | ¼ cup butter-flavored vegetable shortening, cold |
| ½ cup oat bran | |
| ½ teaspoon salt | ¾ cup lowfat buttermilk |
| 1 tablespoon plus 1 teaspoon baking powder | ¼ cup lowfat ricotta cheese |
| | 1 tablespoon honey |
| 2 tablespoons granulated sugar | 2 teaspoons vanilla extract |

Preheat oven to 400 degrees F. Line a cookie sheet with foil or parchment paper.

In a large mixing bowl combine flour, bran, salt, baking powder, and sugar. Add the shortening and rub mixture together with your fingers to completely distribute. Mixture will be coarse. In a separate mixing bowl combine all remaining ingredients and whisk together until smooth. Pour into dry ingredients. Mix with a fork to form a soft dough, being careful not to overwork dough.

Turn dough out onto a lightly floured surface and knead just enough to form a ball. Roll or pat dough into a 9-inch circle. Cut into 10 even wedges using a sharp knife.

Place scones on prepared cookie sheet at least 1 inch apart and bake for 20 to 25 minutes or until scones are light golden brown.

Cool scones completely on a rack and store in an airtight container.

## Each Serving Provides

160 Calories, 34% from Fat, 6 g Fat, 23 g Carbohydrates, 4 g Protein,
84 mg Calcium, 1 g Dietary Fiber, 264 mg Sodium, 3 mg Cholesterol.

# Plain Buttermilk Drop Scones

Split these in half and treat them to your favorite kind of jam just as you would with any other kind of farm-fresh scone!

**10 scones**

| | | | |
|---|---|---|---|
| 2 | cups all-purpose flour | $3/4$ | cup lowfat buttermilk |
| $1/2$ | teaspoon salt | $1/4$ | cup lowfat ricotta cheese |
| 1 | tablespoon plus 1 teaspoon baking powder | $1/4$ | cup 2 percent milk |
| 3 | tablespoons granulated sugar | 1 | tablespoon vanilla extract |
| $1/4$ | cup butter-flavored vegetable shortening, cold | $2^{1/2}$ | tablespoons granulated sugar for tops of scones |

Preheat oven to 400 degrees F. Line a cookie sheet with aluminum foil or parchment paper and lightly coat with vegetable or canola oil spray.

In a large mixing bowl combine flour, salt, baking powder, and 3 tablespoons sugar. Add the shortening and rub mixture together with your fingers to completely distribute. Mixture will be coarse. In a separate mixing bowl combine all remaining ingredients except for sugar, and whisk together until smooth. Pour into dry ingredients and mix with a fork to form a soft dough, being careful not to overwork dough.

Using a large spoon, drop scones onto prepared cookie sheet at least 2 inches apart, and sprinkle the tops with the remaining sugar. Bake for approximately 15 to 20 minutes. Scones should be light golden brown and firm to the touch.

Cool scones completely on a rack and store in an airtight container.

### Each Serving Provides

176 Calories, 30% from Fat, 6 g Fat, 25 g Carbohydrates, 4 g Protein, 91 mg Calcium, 1 g Dietary Fiber, 267 mg Sodium, 4 mg Cholesterol.

# Pumpkin Spice Drop Scones

I love any kind of baked good that has been flavored with pumpkin. These scones are one way you can satisfy your pumpkin pie craving when the holidays are many months away.

**10 scones**

| | | | |
|---|---|---|---|
| 2 | cups all-purpose flour | ¼ | cup butter-flavored vegetable shortening, cold |
| ½ | teaspoon salt | | |
| 1 | tablespoon plus 1 teaspoon baking powder | ¾ | cup lowfat buttermilk |
| 4 | tablespoons granulated sugar | 2 | tablespoons 2 percent milk |
| ½ | teaspoon each:<br>ground nutmeg<br>ground cinnamon<br>ground allspice<br>ground ginger | ½ | cup canned pumpkin |
| | | 1 | tablespoon vanilla extract |

Preheat oven to 400 degrees F. Line a cookie sheet with foil or parchment paper and lightly coat with vegetable or canola oil spray.

In a large mixing bowl combine flour, salt, baking powder, sugar, and spices. Add shortening and completely distribute by rubbing mixture together with your fingers. Mixture will be coarse. In a separate mixing bowl combine all remaining ingredients and whisk together until smooth. Pour into dry ingredients and mix with a fork to form a soft dough, being careful not to overwork dough.

Using a large spoon, drop dough onto prepared cookie sheet, placing scones at least 2 inches apart. Bake for approximately 15 to 20 minutes. Scones should be light golden brown and firm to the touch.

Cool scones completely on a rack and store in an airtight container.

## Each Serving Provides

173 Calories, 28% from Fat, 5 g Fat, 27 g Carbohydrates, 4 g Protein, 58 mg Calcium, 1 g Dietary Fiber, 261 mg Sodium, 1 mg Cholesterol.

# Banana Drop Scones

The addition of a very ripe banana makes these scones exceptionally moist. For an extra treat, try them with the Date Nut Cream Cheese spread (page 135).

**10 scones**

2 cups all-purpose flour
½ teaspoon salt
1 tablespoon plus 1 teaspoon baking powder
1 teaspoon ground cinnamon
1 teaspoon ground allspice
3 tablespoons granulated sugar

¼ cup butter-flavored vegetable shortening, cold
1 medium-sized ripe banana
¾ cup lowfat buttermilk
¼ cup 2 percent milk
2 teaspoons vanilla extract

Preheat oven to 400 degrees F. Line a cookie sheet with foil or parchment paper and lightly coat with vegetable or canola oil spray.

In a large mixing bowl combine flour, salt, baking powder, spices, and sugar. Add the shortening and rub mixture together with your fingers to completely distribute. Mixture will be coarse. Combine the banana, buttermilk, 2 percent milk, and vanilla in a food processor, and puree until smooth. Pour into dry ingredients and mix with a fork to form a soft dough, being careful not to overwork dough.

With a large spoon, drop dough onto prepared cookie sheet, placing scones at least 2 inches apart. Bake for approximately 15 to 20 minutes. Scones should be light golden brown and firm to the touch.

Cool scones completely on a rack, and store in an airtight container.

### Each Serving Provides

176 Calories, 28% from Fat, 5 g Fat, 27 g Carbohydrates, 4 g Protein, 63 mg Calcium, 1 g Dietary Fiber, 263 mg Sodium, 1 mg Cholesterol.

Scones

# Cinnamon Raisin Drop Scones

Cinnamon raisin bread happens to be one of my favorites.
I have noticed many other cinnamon raisin goodies, including
bagels! Yum! So I guess these drop scones will fit right in
with the more traditional favorites.

**10 scones**

Cinnamon sugar topping
2 1/2  tablespoons granulated
       sugar
1  teaspoon ground cinnamon
1/2  teaspoon shortening

Batter
1/2  cup sultanas or raisins
1/3  cup water
1  tablespoon granulated
   sugar
2  cups all-purpose flour

1/2  teaspoon salt
1  tablespoon plus 1 teaspoon
   baking powder
1  teaspoon ground cinnamon
2  tablespoons granulated
   sugar
1/4  cup butter-flavored vege-
     table shortening, cold
3/4  cup lowfat buttermilk
1/4  cup lowfat ricotta cheese
1/2  cup 2 percent milk
1  tablespoon vanilla extract

Preheat oven to 400 degrees F. Line a cookie sheet with foil or
parchment paper and lightly coat with vegetable or canola oil spray.

Prepare topping: Combine all ingredients and rub together to
distribute the shortening. The sugar will appear damp and
crumbly. Set aside.

Prepare batter: In a small saucepan combine raisins, water, and
1 tablespoon sugar, and simmer over medium heat until raisins are
plump and have absorbed the liquid, approximately 10 to 15 minutes. Set aside to cool.

In a large mixing bowl combine flour, salt, baking powder, cinnamon, and 2 tablespoons sugar. Add shortening and completely
distribute by rubbing mixture together with your fingers. Mixture
will be coarse. Toss in the cooled raisins. In a separate mixing bowl
combine all remaining ingredients and whisk together until
smooth. Pour into the dry ingredients and mix with a fork to form a
soft dough, being careful not to overwork the dough.

With a large spoon, drop dough onto prepared cookie sheet, placing scones at least 2 inches apart. Sprinkle the top of each scone with some of the cinnamon sugar, and bake for approximately 15 to 20 minutes.

Cool scones completely on a rack and store in an airtight container.

### Each Serving Provides

214 Calories, 26% from Fat, 6 g Fat, 34 g Carbohydrates, 5 g Protein,
106 mg Calcium, 1 g Dietary Fiber, 270 mg Sodium, 5 mg Cholesterol.

# Cranberry Drop Scones

These are made with fresh cranberries for a deliciously tart taste. Mark your calendar in November and remind yourself to buy a few extra bags of cranberries for the freezer— you'll want to make these in the off-season!

**10 scones**

3/4 cup fresh cranberries (or thawed frozen ones)

2 tablespoons granulated sugar

2 cups all-purpose flour

1/2 teaspoon salt

1 tablespoon plus 1 teaspoon baking powder

2 tablespoons granulated sugar

1/4 cup butter-flavored vegetable shortening, cold

3/4 cup lowfat buttermilk

1/4 cup lowfat ricotta cheese

1/4 cup 2 percent milk

1 tablespoon grated orange peel

1 tablespoon vanilla extract

2 1/2 tablespoons granulated sugar for tops of scones

Preheat oven to 400 degrees F. Line a cookie sheet with foil or parchment paper and lightly coat with vegetable or canola oil spray.

Put cranberries in a food processor and process until they are coarse, but not pureed. Transfer chopped cranberries to a bowl and mix with 2 tablespoons sugar. Set aside.

In a large mixing bowl combine flour, salt, baking powder, and 2 tablespoons sugar. Add shortening and completely distribute by rubbing mixture together with your fingers. Mixture will be coarse. Toss the sugared cranberries in the flour mixture (this keeps your scones from coming out too pink because the flour coats the bits of cranberries and keeps the juice from running). In a separate mixing bowl combine all remaining ingredients except the sugar, and whisk together until smooth. Pour into dry ingredients and mix with a fork, being careful not to overwork the dough.

With a large spoon, drop dough onto prepared cookie sheet, placing scones at least 2 inches apart, and sprinkle the tops with the remaining sugar. Bake for approximately 15 to 20 minutes. Scones should be light golden brown and firm to the touch.

Cool scones completely on a rack and store in an airtight container.

### Each Serving Provides
185 Calories, 29% from Fat, 6 g Fat, 28 g Carbohydrates, 4 g Protein, 92 mg Calcium, 1 g Dietary Fiber, 267 mg Sodium, 4 mg Cholesterol.

Scones

# Breakfast Breads and Coffee Cakes

If you have ever stayed at a hotel or a bed-and-breakfast that served a continental breakfast or afternoon tea, then you know how special coffee cakes and breakfast breads can be. They are just as wonderful to serve in the morning as muffins, and just as easy to make. This is the chapter you'll find yourself turning to when company is coming, especially if you're entertaining overnight guests. Make a couple of these breads and put out your finest teapot and cups. You're sure to make a lasting impression. But don't forget to pamper yourself, too. Why not bake some, pack them up, and take them along on a picnic, an overnight trip, or a simple drive in the country?

## Baking Tips

When it comes to combining the ingredients and mixing them, you will find that coffee cakes and breakfast breads are made in much the same way as muffins. The trick is not to overmix the batter. Use a rubber spatula to combine the wet and dry ingredients only to the point at which all the ingredients are just moistened, so that you don't overwork the batter. Unlike muffins, the baking temperature of coffee cakes and tea breads is the standard 350 degees F.

# Apricot Lemon Tea Bread

This delicious bread actually has fresh brewed tea in it, which is what gives it such an interesting flavor. The taste of tea combines beautifully with the sweet tartness of the apricots.

**20 servings**

1 cup dried apricots, quartered
1 cup water
$\frac{1}{4}$ cup granulated sugar
3 cups all-purpose flour
1 cup granulated sugar
1 tablespoon baking powder
$\frac{1}{2}$ teaspoon salt
1 tablespoon grated lemon peel
$\frac{1}{3}$ cup lowfat buttermilk

$\frac{1}{2}$ cup 2 percent milk
1 cup strong, fresh brewed tea such as orange pekoe, cooled to room temperature
$\frac{1}{4}$ cup canola oil
1 large egg white
2 teaspoons vanilla extract
1 tablespoon fresh lemon juice

In a small saucepan combine apricots, water, and $\frac{1}{4}$ cup sugar. Cook over medium-high heat for 10 to 15 minutes, until apricots are tender and most of the liquid has been absorbed. Set aside to cool.

Preheat oven to 350 degrees F. Lightly coat two 8 × 3$\frac{3}{4}$-inch loaf pans with vegetable or canola oil spray.

In a large mixing bowl combine flour, 1 cup sugar, baking powder, salt, and lemon peel. In a separate mixing bowl combine all remaining ingredients and whisk together until smooth. Stir in cooled apricots and any remaining liquid in the pan. Pour into dry ingredients and mix just until all ingredients are moist.

Pour batter into prepared pans and bake for 35 to 40 minutes or until a cake tester inserted into the center comes out clean.

Cool in pans on a rack for 5 minutes before inverting onto a rack to cool completely. Store in an airtight container.

### Each Serving Provides

166 Calories, 17% from Fat, 3 g Fat, 32 g Carbohydrates, 3 g Protein, 31 mg Calcium, 1 g Dietary Fiber, 116 mg Sodium, 1 mg Cholesterol.

# Cherry Orange Loaves

Everybody loves cherries, or at least most of us do. I know
I am particularly fond of them, especially when they are in season.
Unfortunately the cherry season is very short, and often at the
mercy of the weather. So here's a recipe that you can make
year-round using good quality canned cherry filling.
I recommend Comstock filling.

**20 servings**

| | |
|---|---|
| 2¾ cups all-purpose flour | ¾ cup orange juice |
| ½ cup whole wheat flour | 3 tablespoons canola oil |
| ¾ cup granulated sugar | 2 large egg whites |
| 1 tablespoon baking powder | 1 tablespoon vanilla extract |
| ½ teaspoon salt | 2 tablespoons grated orange |
| ⅓ cup lowfat buttermilk | peel |
| ½ cup 2 percent milk | 1½ cup canned cherry pie filling |

Preheat oven to 350 degrees F. Lightly coat two 8 × 3¾-inch loaf
pans with vegetable or canola oil spray.

In a large mixing bowl combine both flours, sugar, baking powder, and salt. In a separate mixing bowl combine all remaining ingredients except for cherry filling and whisk together until smooth.
Stir in cherry filling and pour into dry ingredients. Mix just until all
ingredients are moist.

Pour batter into prepared pans and bake for 35 to 45 minutes
or until a cake tester inserted into the center comes out clean.

Cool in pans on a rack for 5 minutes before inverting onto a
rack to cool completely. Store in an airtight container.

### Each Serving Provides

145 Calories, 17% from Fat, 3 g Fat, 27 g Carbohydrates, 3 g Protein,
29 mg Calcium, 2 g Dietary Fiber, 117 mg Sodium, 1 mg Cholesterol.

# Cranberry Rhubarb Bread

I have heard of cranberries being combined with just about anything you can imagine—oranges, strawberries, and apples are popular choices. I wanted to do something completely different, so I decided to try rhubarb. This bread is surprisingly delicious! These two flavors were meant to be together.

**20 servings**

1 (12-ounce) bag of fresh cranberries
2 (14-inch-long) stalks of fresh rhubarb, cut into $^1/_2$-inch pieces
$^1/_2$ cup granulated sugar
$^1/_3$ cup orange juice
2 $^3/_4$ cups all-purpose flour
$^1/_2$ cup whole wheat flour

$^3/_4$ cup granulated sugar
1 tablespoon baking powder
$^1/_2$ teaspoon salt
1 teaspoon ground ginger
$^1/_3$ cup lowfat buttermilk
$^3/_4$ cup orange juice
$^1/_4$ cup canola oil
1 large egg white
1 tablespoon vanilla extract

Preheat oven to 350 degrees F. Lightly coat two 8 × 3 $^3/_4$-inch loaf pans with vegetable or canola oil spray.

In a medium-sized saucepan combine cranberries, rhubarb, $^1/_2$ cup sugar, and orange juice, and cook over medium-high heat, stirring occasionally, until cranberries begin to pop and rhubarb is tender, approximately 10 minutes. Set aside to cool.

In a large mixing bowl combine both flours, $^3/_4$ cup sugar, baking powder, salt, and ground ginger. In a separate mixing bowl combine all remaining ingredients except cranberry-rhubarb mixture, and whisk together until smooth. Stir in cooled cranberry mixture and pour into dry ingredients. Mix just until all ingredients are moist.

Pour batter into prepared pans and bake for approximately 35 to 45 minutes or until a cake tester inserted into the center comes out clean.

Cool in pans on a rack for 5 minutes before inverting onto a rack to cool completely. Store in an airtight container.

### Each Serving Provides

168 Calories, 17% from Fat, 3 g Fat, 33 g Carbohydrates, 3 g Protein,
27 mg Calcium, 2 g Dietary Fiber, 112 mg Sodium, 0 mg Cholesterol.

# Banana Nut Bread

I can never resist slicing into a loaf of banana bread . . . nor can I
stop eating it! For the best tasting bread use the ripest bananas,
ones that have turned mostly black on the outside. These will
deliver an intense banana flavor and a luscious texture.

**20 servings**

| | |
|---|---|
| 2 1/2  cups all-purpose flour | 1/3  cup lowfat buttermilk |
| 1/2  cup granulated sugar | 1 1/2  medium-sized ripe bananas |
| 1/2  cup brown sugar, firmly | 1/3  cup 2 percent milk |
| packed | 1/3  cup lowfat ricotta cheese |
| 1  teaspoon salt | 2  tablespoons honey |
| 1  tablespoon baking powder | 2  large egg whites |
| 1  teaspoon baking soda | 2  tablespoons canola oil |
| 1  teaspoon ground allspice | 1  tablespoon vanilla extract |
| 1  teaspoon ground cinnamon | |
| 1/2  cup (1 1/2 ounces) finely | |
| ground walnuts | |

Preheat oven to 350 degrees F. Lightly coat two 8 × 3 3/4-inch loaf
pans with vegetable or canola oil spray.

In a large mixing bowl combine flour, both sugars, salt, baking
powder, baking soda, spices, and ground walnuts. In a food processor combine the buttermilk and banana, and puree until smooth.
In a separate mixing bowl combine the 2 percent milk, ricotta,
honey, egg whites, oil, and vanilla extract. Add the banana puree
and whisk together until smooth. Pour into dry ingredients, and
mix just until all ingredients are moist.

Pour batter into prepared pans and bake for approximately 35
to 40 minutes or until a cake tester inserted into the center comes
out clean.

Cool in pans on a rack for 5 minutes before inverting onto a
rack to cool completely. Store in an airtight container.

Each Serving Provides

162 Calories, 22% from Fat, 4 g Fat, 28 g Carbohydrates, 4 g Protein,
56 mg Calcium, 9 g Dietary Fiber, 231 mg Sodium, 2 mg Cholesterol.

# Fresh Peach Lime Bread

I make fresh peach lime salsa when peaches are in season, and it's great served with grilled fish or chicken. That salsa was my inspiration for this refreshing breakfast bread. This is the perfect bread to take along on a summer picnic!

**20 servings**

| | | | |
|---|---|---|---|
| 1 | tablespoon cold water | 2½ | cups all-purpose flour |
| 1 | tablespoon cornstarch | ¾ | cup granulated sugar |
| 2 | medium-sized peaches, firm but ripe, pitted and cut into ¼-inch pieces | 1 | tablespoon baking powder |
| | | 1 | teaspoon baking soda |
| ¼ | cup fresh lime juice | ½ | teaspoon salt |
| 2 | tablespoons grated lime peel | ½ | cup lowfat buttermilk |
| | | ½ | cup 2 percent milk |
| 2 | tablespoons granulated sugar | 3 | tablespoons canola oil |
| | | 2 | large egg whites |
| | | 2 | teaspoons vanilla extract |

Preheat oven to 350 degrees F. Lightly coat two 8 × 3¾-inch loaf pans with vegetable or canola oil spray.

Combine water and cornstarch and set aside. In a medium-sized saucepan combine peaches, lime juice, lime peel, and 2 tablespoons sugar. Cook over medium-high heat until peaches are tender, but not mushy, and mixture is juicy. Add the dissolved cornstarch and stir to distribute. Continue to cook for an additional minute until thickened. Set aside to cool.

In a large mixing bowl combine flour, ¾ cup sugar, baking powder, baking soda, and salt. In a separate mixing bowl combine remaining ingredients and whisk together until smooth. Stir in the cooled peaches until combined, and pour into dry ingredients. Mix just until all ingredients are moist.

Pour batter into prepared pans and bake for 35 to 40 minutes or until a cake tester inserted into the center comes out clean.

Cool in pans on a rack for 5 minutes before inverting onto a rack to cool completely. Store in an airtight container.

### Each Serving Provides

123 Calories, 18% from Fat, 3 g Fat, 23 g Carbohydrates, 3 g Protein, 30 mg Calcium, 1 g Dietary Fiber, 176 mg Sodium, 1 mg Cholesterol.

# Pumpkin Maple and Pecan Bread

I love baking with pumpkin. This is a great holiday bread.
The maple and pumpkin make for a magical combination
and the pecans are the icing on the cake!

### 20 servings

2 1/2 cups all-purpose flour
1/2 cup granulated sugar
1/4 cup brown sugar, firmly packed
1/2 teaspoon salt
1 tablespoon baking powder
1 teaspoon baking soda
1 teaspoon ground allspice
1 teaspoon ground cinnamon
1/2 cup ground toasted pecans
3/4 cup canned pumpkin
1/3 cup lowfat buttermilk
1/2 cup 2 percent milk
1/2 cup pure maple syrup
1 tablespoon canola oil
1 large whole egg plus 1 egg white
1 tablespoon vanilla extract

Preheat oven to 350 degrees F. Lightly coat two 8 × 3 3/4-inch loaf pans with vegetable or canola oil spray.

In a large mixing bowl combine flour, both sugars, salt, baking powder, baking soda, spices, and pecans. In a separate mixing bowl combine all remaining ingredients and whisk together until smooth. Pour into dry ingredients and mix just until all ingredients are moist.

Pour batter into prepared pans and bake for approximately 35 to 45 minutes or until a cake tester inserted into the center comes out clean.

Cool in pans on a rack for 5 minutes before inverting onto a rack to cool completely. Store in an airtight container.

### Each Serving Provides

151 Calories, 20% from Fat, 3 g Fat, 27 g Carbohydrates, 3 g Protein,
43 mg Calcium, 1 g Dietary Fiber, 176 mg Sodium, 11 mg Cholesterol.

# Caribbean Yam and Coconut Bread

I love Caribbean food, and I cook it often, especially for
summer dinner parties. Thus the inspiration for this recipe.
Even if you've never been to the Caribbean, you can still
get a little taste of the islands in this bread.

**20 servings**

| | |
|---|---|
| 1 medium-sized yam, peeled and cut into 1-inch chunks | 1 tablespoon baking powder |
| ½ cup orange juice | 1 tablespoon grated lime peel |
| 3 cups all-purpose flour | ¾ cup sweetened flaked coconut |
| ¾ cup brown sugar, firmly packed | ½ cup lowfat buttermilk |
| ¼ cup granulated sugar | 1 cup 2 percent milk |
| 1 teaspoon ground allspice | 3 tablespoons canola oil |
| ½ teaspoon salt | 1 large egg white |
| | 1 tablespoon vanilla extract |

Preheat oven to 350 degrees F. Lightly coat two 8 × 3¾-inch loaf
pans with vegetable or canola oil spray.

Place cut yam in a medium-sized saucepan and add enough
water to cover. Cook over medium-high heat until tender. Drain off
the water and set aside to cool.

When the yam is cool, place in a food processor along with
orange juice, and puree until smooth. You should have approximately 1½ cups of puree. If you are a little short, add enough
orange juice to bring it up to 1½ cups.

In a large mixing bowl combine flour, both sugars, allspice,
salt, baking powder, lime peel, and coconut. In a separate mixing
bowl combine all remaining ingredients, including the yam puree,
and whisk together until smooth. Pour into dry ingredients and
mix just until all ingredients are moist.

Pour batter into prepared pans and bake for approximately 40
to 50 minutes or until a cake tester inserted into the center comes
out clean.

Cool in pans on a rack for 5 minutes before inverting onto a
rack to cool completely. Store in an airtight container.

### Each Serving Provides

171 Calories, 21% from Fat, 4 g Fat, 31 g Carbohydrates, 3 g Protein,
45 mg Calcium, 1 g Dietary Fiber, 133 mg Sodium, 1 mg Cholesterol.

# Sweet Parsnip Coffee Cake with Cream Cheese Icing

Don't be so quick to cast aside this delicious cousin to the carrot. The parsnip is often overlooked in favor of its more popular cousin, but I believe a revival is afoot. I have created many different dishes with parsnips, all of which are wonderful, so trying them out in the baking department seemed like an obvious step. This coffee cake is absolute proof of their charm and the sweet taste that they impart to a recipe.

**12 servings**

Cake

- 2 cups all-purpose flour
- 3/4 cup granulated sugar
- 3/4 teaspoon salt
- 1 tablespoon baking powder
- 1 teaspoon ground cardamom
- 1/2 teaspoon ground cinnamon
- 1/2 cup lowfat buttermilk
- 1/2 cup 2 percent milk
- 1/3 cup lowfat ricotta cheese
- 1 large egg plus 1 large egg white
- 2 tablespoons canola oil
- 1 tablespoon vanilla extract
- 1 cup finely grated parsnips*

Icing

- 1 cup powdered sugar
- 1 tablespoon 2 percent milk
- 1 teaspoon vanilla extract
- 2 tablespoons light Neufchâtel cheese, room temperature

Preheat oven to 350 degrees F. Lightly coat an 8 × 8 × 2-inch square baking pan with vegetable or canola oil spray.

Prepare cake: In a large mixing bowl combine flour, sugar, salt, baking powder, and spices. In a separate mixing bowl combine all remaining ingredients except for parsnips, and whisk together until smooth. Stir in parsnips and pour into dry ingredients. Mix together just until all ingredients are moist.

* It is best to choose parsnips that are small because they are the most tender. If you are using larger ones, be sure to remove the woody and fibrous core before grating them.

Pour batter into prepared pan and bake for approximately 40 to 50 minutes or until a cake tester inserted into the center comes out clean. Cool completely in pan, on a rack before icing.

Prepare icing: Combine all ingredients in a small mixing bowl and beat on medium speed with an electric mixer until smooth and creamy. Spread evenly over cooled cake.

Store cake in an airtight container.

### Each Serving Provides

215 Calories, 16% from Fat, 4 g Fat, 40 g Carbohydrates, 5 g Protein,
87 mg Calcium, 1 g Dietary Fiber, 247 mg Sodium, 21 mg Cholesterol.

# Apple Spice Coffee Cake

This coffee cake tastes as delicious and down-home as it sounds. With hints of cinnamon and nutmeg and two layers of fresh apples, this cake is perfect for a chilly winter morning.

**12 servings**

2 medium-sized Granny Smith apples, peeled, cored, and cut into $\frac{1}{8}$-inch slices
1 teaspoon fresh lemon juice
2 tablespoons brown sugar
1 teaspoon ground ginger
1$\frac{1}{2}$ cups all-purpose flour
$\frac{1}{2}$ cup whole wheat flour
$\frac{3}{4}$ cup granulated sugar
$\frac{3}{4}$ teaspoon salt
1 tablespoon baking powder
1 teaspoon each:
 ground cinnamon
 ground cloves
 ground nutmeg

$\frac{1}{2}$ cup lowfat buttermilk
$\frac{1}{2}$ cup 2 percent milk
$\frac{1}{2}$ cup lowfat ricotta cheese
1 large whole egg plus 1 egg white
3 tablespoons canola oil
1 tablespoon vanilla extract
2 tablespoons granulated sugar for top of cake

Preheat oven to 350 degrees F. Lightly coat an 8 × 8 × 2-inch square baking pan with vegetable or canola oil spray.

Toss the apples with the lemon juice, brown sugar, and ginger, and set aside.

In a large mixing bowl combine both flours, $\frac{3}{4}$ cup sugar, salt, baking powder, and spices. In a separate mixing bowl combine all remaining ingredients, except for apples and 2 tablespoons sugar, and whisk together until smooth. Pour into dry ingredients and mix just until all ingredients are moist.

Pour half of the batter into prepared pan and smooth with a spatula. Cover the batter with half of the apple slices in an even layer, and cover them with the remaining batter, smoothing the top. Cover with the remaining apple slices in an even layer, and sprinkle the entire surface with the remaining 2 tablespoons sugar.

Bake for approximately 40 to 50 minutes or until a cake tester inserted into the center comes out clean.

Cool completely in pan on a rack. Store cake in an airtight container.

## Hints

You can make this cake even more wonderful by adding $1/2$ cup of chopped raisins or sultanas to the batter. If you really want to do it up, frost it with the cream cheese icing that is used on the Sweet Parsnip Coffee Cake!

For a larger-sized piece of cake that is not as high, bake this coffee cake in a 9 × 13-inch baking pan. There will not be enough apples to do two layers so just layer them on top, or add another apple and make two layers. The baking time will decrease by as much as 20 minutes.

### Each Serving Provides

219 Calories, 22% from Fat, 6 g Fat, 38 g Carbohydrates, 5 g Protein,
105 mg Calcium, 2 g Dietary Fiber, 249 mg Sodium, 22 mg Cholesterol.

# Blueberry Cornmeal Coffee Cake with Streusel and Lemon Icing

Moist and crisp, sweet and tart, this cake delivers a combination of flavors and textures that should please any palate. Bursting with blueberries, the moist cake is topped by crisp streusel and a tart lemon icing that brings it all together—beautifully.

**12 servings**

## Streusel

- 1/3 cup brown sugar, firmly packed
- 1/2 cup all-purpose flour
- 2 tablespoons light butter, melted

## Batter

- 1 1/4 cups all-purpose flour
- 1/4 cup masa (fine cornmeal)
- 1/2 cup granulated sugar
- 1 teaspoon salt
- 1 tablespoon baking powder
- 1/2 cup lowfat buttermilk
- 1/2 cup 2 percent milk
- 1/3 cup honey
- 1 large whole egg plus 1 egg white
- 2 tablespoons canola oil
- 2 teaspoons vanilla extract
- 1 1/4 cups blueberries, fresh or frozen

## Lemon Icing

- 1 cup powdered sugar
- 1 tablespoon fresh lemon juice
- 2 teaspoons grated lemon peel
- 1/4 teaspoon vanilla extract
- 1 1/2 teaspoons water

Preheat oven to 350 degrees F. Lightly coat a 9 × 13-inch baking pan with vegetable or canola oil spray.

Prepare streusel: Combine all ingredients in a small mixing bowl and rub together with your fingers to make coarse crumbs. Set aside.

Prepare batter: In a large mixing bowl combine flour, masa, sugar, salt, and baking powder. In a separate mixing bowl combine all remaining ingredients except for blueberries, and whisk together until smooth. Toss the blueberries in the flour mixture and then pour in the wet ingredients, mixing just until all ingredients are moist.

Pour batter into prepared baking pan. Smooth the top with a spatula and sprinkle the surface evenly with the streusel. Bake for approximately 25 to 30 minutes or until a cake tester inserted into the center comes out clean.

Cool completely in pan before icing.

Prepare icing: Combine all ingredients in a small mixing bowl and stir with a spoon until smooth. If icing is too thick, you may add a little more water to get a smoother consistency. Drizzle icing over cooled cake.

Store in an airtight container.

### Each Serving Provides

245 Calories, 16% from Fat, 4 g Fat, 49 g Carbohydrates, 4 g Protein,
53 mg Calcium, 1 g Dietary Fiber, 300 mg Sodium, 22 mg Cholesterol.

# Cinnamon Orange Coffee Ring

The intense orange flavor of this cake is accented by just the right amount of cinnamon. This cake is as lovely to look at as it is delightful to eat. It is made in a round bundt pan, which gives it a formal look, and the icing drizzling over the top and flowing down the sides is the perfect finishing touch.

**12 servings**

Batter

- 1 cup orange juice, preferably fresh
- 2 cups all-purpose flour
- ¾ cup granulated sugar
- ¾ teaspoon salt
- 1 tablespoon baking powder
- 1½ teaspoons ground cinnamon
- ½ cup lowfat buttermilk
- ⅓ cup lowfat ricotta cheese
- 1 large whole egg plus 1 egg white
- 2 tablespoons grated orange peel
- 2 tablespoons canola oil
- 1 tablespoon vanilla extract

Icing

- 1¼ cups powdered sugar
- 2 tablespoons orange juice

Preheat oven to 350 degrees F. Lightly coat an 8-inch round bundt or tube pan with vegetable or canola oil spray.

Pour the orange juice into a medium-sized saucepan and simmer over medium-high heat until it is reduced to ½ cup, approximately 10 minutes. Set aside to cool.

In a large mixing bowl combine flour, sugar, salt, baking powder, and cinnamon. In a separate mixing bowl combine all remaining ingredients, including the cooled orange juice, and whisk together until smooth. Pour into dry ingredients and mix just until all ingredients are moist.

Pour batter into prepared pan and bake for approximately 35 to 40 minutes or until a cake tester inserted into the center comes out clean.

Cool cake in pan for 5 minutes and then invert onto a cake rack to cool completely before icing.

Prepare icing: Combine both ingredients in a small mixing bowl and stir until smooth. If icing is too thick, you may add a little more orange juice to get a smoother consistency.

Transfer cake to a serving plate and drizzle icing over top, letting it flow down the sides.

Store in an airtight container.

### Each Serving Provides

216 Calories, 15% from Fat, 4 g Fat, 42 g Carbohydrates, 4 g Protein, 73 mg Calcium, 1 g Dietary Fiber, 240 mg Sodium, 20 mg Cholesterol.

# Caramel Pecan Coffee Cake

Even though this is a lower fat cookbook, you will find that the amount of fat does vary from recipe to recipe. The majority of the recipes are reasonably low in fat, but there are a few instances, such as this one, where a bit more creeps in for those times when you really want to be decadent. I just couldn't resist including this coffee cake, baked upside-down style, because caramel pecan is such a popular combination in its fattening form. I did manage to give a bit and take a bit in order to come up with a fantastic lowfat stand-in. Enjoy that caramel pecan topping—you deserve it!

**12 servings**

Caramel pecan topping
- 1 tablespoon butter-flavored vegetable shortening
- 1/2 tablespoon real butter
- 1 tablespoon honey
- 1/2 cup brown sugar, firmly packed
- 1/3 cup finely chopped pecans

Batter
- 2 cups all-purpose flour
- 1/2 cup plus 2 tablespoons granulated sugar
- 3/4 teaspoon salt
- 1 tablespoon baking powder
- 1/2 teaspoon ground allspice
- 1/2 cup 2 percent milk
- 1/2 cup lowfat buttermilk
- 1/3 cup lowfat ricotta
- 1 large whole egg plus 1 egg white
- 1 tablespoon vanilla extract
- 1 tablespoon canola oil

Preheat oven to 350 degrees F.

Prepare topping: Place an 8 × 2-inch round cake pan over medium heat and add the shortening and butter. When melted add the honey and brown sugar and stir until the sugar is melted. At first it will be lumped together, but as it melts it will spread out to cover the bottom of the pan. Remove from heat and sprinkle the pecans evenly over the sugar. Set aside to cool.

Prepare batter: In a large mixing bowl combine flour, sugar, salt, baking powder, and allspice. In a separate mixing bowl combine all remaining ingredients and whisk together until smooth. Pour into dry ingredients and mix just until all ingredients are moist.

Pour batter into prepared pan, over the cooled caramel pecan bottom, and bake for approximately 35 to 45 minutes or until a toothpick inserted into the center comes out clean.

Cool in pan for 5 minutes then immediately invert onto a plate. Some of the caramel pecan topping may stick to the bottom of the pan. If so, simply use a small metal spatula to place it back on the cake.

Cool before cutting, and store in an airtight container.

### Each Serving Provides

233 Calories, 24% from Fat, 6 g Fat, 39 g Carbohydrates, 5 g Protein, 88 mg Calcium, 1 g Dietary Fiber, 254 mg Sodium, 22 mg Cholesterol.

# Zucchini Bread

Fresh grated zucchini is the magic here. This bread can't help
but be moist and delicious.

**20 servings**

| | |
|---|---|
| 2 1/2 cups all-purpose flour | 1/3 cup lowfat buttermilk |
| 1/2 cup granulated sugar | 1/2 cup 2 percent milk |
| 1/2 cup brown sugar, firmly packed | 1/3 cup lowfat ricotta cheese |
| 1/2 teaspoon salt | 2 tablespoons honey |
| 1 tablespoon baking powder | 1 large whole egg plus 1 egg white |
| 1 teaspoon baking soda | 1 tablespoon vanilla extract |
| 1 teaspoon ground allspice | 1/4 cup canola oil |
| 1 teaspoon ground cinnamon | 1 1/4 cups grated zucchini |

Preheat oven to 350 degrees F. Lightly coat two 8 × 3 3/4-inch loaf
pans with vegetable or canola oil spray.

In a large mixing bowl combine flour, both sugars, salt, baking
powder, baking soda, and spices. In a separate mixing bowl combine all remaining ingredients and whisk together until smooth.
Pour into dry ingredients and mix just until all ingredients are
moist.

Pour into prepared pans and bake for approximately 35 to 40
minutes or until a cake tester inserted into the center comes out
clean.

Cool in pans on a rack for 5 minutes before inverting onto a
rack to cool completely. Store in an airtight container.

### Each Serving Provides

151 Calories, 22% from Fat, 4 g Fat, 26 g Carbohydrates, 3 g Protein,
57 mg Calcium, 1 g Dietary Fiber, 179 mg Sodium, 13 mg Cholesterol.

# Hotcakes and Waffles

Let's face it, nothing brings you home like a hot stack of fluffy pancakes doused with gooey, delicious syrup. Then there are those heavenly waffles—imagine Belgian waffles, flavored with hazelnuts and topped with fresh fruits and cream. No, it's not a dream. These goodies and a variety of others can be yours faster than you can say "Pass that syrup!"

Pancakes and waffles can be frighteningly high in fat and calories, which is part of why they taste so irresistibly delicious! However, it is possible to make pancakes that are lower in fat without sacrificing their wonderful taste and texture. Most of the fat in pancakes is completely unnecessary. Aside from the amount of oil or melted butter in the batter itself, many of us have a habit of over-oiling the pan or griddle that we use to cook them, which adds extra fat and calories. Then there's the worst culprit of all, the butter that gets slathered (if you're like me) between each and every pancake! I confess, I am never going to banish all the butter from my hotcakes, but I've figured out how to exercise some self-restraint. It helps to have some options, as you will soon discover in this chapter. Remember, change is good; you just have to have an open mind.

## Helpful Hotcake Tips

### EQUIPMENT

I think most of us are guilty of making our pancakes in some pretty sad-looking pans. Most of us grab whatever pan is in the kitchen at the time and not dirty or otherwise engaged. And I'll admit, the pancakes come out all right—most of the time—and are, for the most part, reasonably edible. But they couldn't have gotten any further from perfect if they had sprouted legs and learned to run!

What do I mean by perfect? Oh, just about every pancake in the world other than mine. Think of those disgustingly perfect IHOP pancakes, so nice and golden and round, without a single burnt spot. . . . Of course, to achieve this kind of sublime perfection you will need to rip out half of your kitchen and install a gas-flame-heated professional griddle. I don't know about you, but I don't foresee this kind of project anywhere in my near future!

So short of remodeling, what can you do about those uneven, imperfect, and almost always lopsided hotcakes? To set yourself on the path to pancake success, you must resist all urges to use the household frying pan, especially the one that's begun to warp and sink in the middle. If you insist on using a frying pan, invest in one that is heavy-duty cast iron or anodized steel. It should be flat and shallow and as large in circumference as your burner can accommodate. This is not the ideal way to make your pancakes since you can often make only one large pancake or two smaller ones at a time, but nevertheless, it works.

If you don't mind investing a little in a piece of worthwhile equipment, I strongly suggest purchasing a cast-iron griddle made for the stove top. This is the ideal pancake tool and is as close to what the restaurants use as you're going to get at home. If you are one of the lucky ones, you already have Grandma's or even Great Grandma's old cast-iron griddle with its smooth non-stick surface that has been seasoned perfectly from years of use.

Your pancakes must be divine! For those of you less fortunate, do not despair. You can buy a griddle without spending too much money. I paid less than $15.00 for mine. It is a nice, heavy cast-iron design that measures around 18 inches long and 9 inches wide. It sits perfectly across two stove burners, which gives me plenty of space to flip those hotcakes—more than one at a time!—and it is not so big that I'm left wondering where in the heck to put it when it's not in use. If you buy one, be sure to read the instructions on seasoning the griddle before you actually use it. This crucial step creates the classic nonstick surface that is synonymous with cast ironware. There are, of course, griddles made with a nonstick surface such as Teflon. These are also wonderful to use, though they do cost more than the plain cast iron.

If you find that your griddle or pan needs lubrication, avoid using the nonstick cooking sprays, as I have found that they tend to burn on the constantly hot surface. It is better to brush the surface lightly with vegetable or canola oil using a pastry brush.

## Pancake Perfection

It is impossible to give a general temperature setting and precise cooking time for pancakes because there are so many variables, from the thickness of the batter to what you are cooking the pancakes on to what type of stove you are using. My hotcakes come out beautifully on the medium setting of an electric stove. You may have to experiment a bit with the heat to find the optimum temperature on your stove top.

The real trick is to watch the pancakes as they cook and learn when it's time to flip them. Once the batter is poured onto the pan or griddle, the pancake needs a certain amount of time to cook without the bottom half burning first. Perhaps this is where patience can really be a virtue. Watch carefully and the pancake will tell you when it is ready to be flipped: its surface will be covered with bubbles, and the edges will be starting to brown. If you need to, you can peek under the edge by very carefully lifting it up with the tip of your spatula to see how far along it actually is.

If the griddle is too hot, the pancake will be burnt on the bottom when you flip it, regardless of whether you were patient enough to wait for the bubbles to appear on the top. But don't kid yourself into thinking that you can just flip a pancake sooner before it burns. If you do this, not only will your pancake be completely deformed, but the batter will splatter, and you may find yourself wearing some of it.

If your pancakes are burning on the bottom, lower the heat. You may be surprised at how low you may need to go to get it just right. Once you find that perfect temperature setting, and conquer your urge to flip the pancakes too early, you'll find pancakes to be a snap!

## Helpful Waffle Tips

Waffles are a hot item these days. You'll find them on almost every breakfast menu, and now it is even commonplace to find waffle cones for your ice cream. When I was younger, I always passed up the waffles in order to have pancakes. Then I got older and found out what I had been missing.

### WAFFLE IRONS

If you don't already own an electric waffle iron, you can purchase one at almost any department store. Be sure to shop around since prices vary quite a bit from store to store. Waffle irons come in all different shapes and sizes, from the traditional large round Belgian style with four divided sections to a square version. I have even seen waffle irons that make heart-shaped waffles! You can choose one that will best suit your needs and the size of your family. I have a nice compact model made by Oster that makes two perfect 4-inch-square waffles at a time, and then folds up neatly so I can stash it under the cupboard.

## Wondrous Waffles

Waffles are much easier to master than pancakes because the iron does all the work for you. Maybe that's why I like them so much.

The waffle iron will regulate the temperature, all you have to do is determine how much batter you need to add to the iron for each waffle. My waffle iron makes two 4-inch-square waffles at a time, and this is the basis for my recipe yields. The recipe yields may vary depending on the size and shape of your waffle iron.

# Lemon Poppy-Seed Hotcakes

I created these hotcakes with the sole intention of dousing them in Raspberry Syrup (page 123) for a totally different, deliciously decadent breakfast experience. They are light and lemony, and the crunchy poppy seeds are a delightful and unexpected addition to the flapjack repertoire.

**8 hotcakes**

1 1/2  cups all-purpose flour
   4  tablespoons granulated
      sugar
   1  tablespoon baking powder
 1/2  teaspoon salt
   1  tablespoon poppy seeds
   1  cup lowfat buttermilk
 1/2  cup 2 percent milk

   1  tablespoon fresh lemon
      juice
1 1/2  tablespoons grated lemon
      peel
   1  large whole egg
   1  tablespoon canola oil
   1  teaspoon vanilla extract

In a large mixing bowl combine the flour, sugar, baking powder, salt, and poppy seeds. In a separate mixing bowl combine all remaining ingredients and whisk together until smooth. Pour into dry ingredients and whisk together to make a smooth batter.

Pour approximately 1/3 cup batter for each hotcake onto a hot nonstick griddle or pan, using a ladle or large spoon. Turn the hotcakes over when there are bubbles across the top and the edges are beginning to brown. Hotcakes should be golden brown and will spring back when touched.

### Each Serving Provides

165 Calories, 21% from Fat, 4 g Fat, 27 g Carbohydrates, 5 g Protein, 101 mg Calcium, 1 g Dietary Fiber, 308 mg Sodium, 30 mg Cholesterol.

# Old-Fashioned Buttermilk Hotcakes

This basic recipe is perfect for building any number of
scrumptious variations simply by adding a few ingredients.
Some easy variations follow, but don't stop with these
if you have ideas of your own!

**8 hotcakes**

| | | | |
|---|---|---|---|
| 1 1/2 | cups all-purpose flour | 1 | cup lowfat buttermilk |
| 2 | tablespoons granulated sugar | 1/2 | cup 2 percent milk |
| 1 | tablespoon baking powder | 1 | large whole egg |
| 1/2 | teaspoon salt | 1 | tablespoon canola oil |
| | | 2 | teaspoons vanilla extract |

In a large mixing bowl combine flour, sugar, baking powder, and
salt. In a separate mixing bowl combine all remaining ingredients
and whisk together until smooth. Pour into the dry ingredients and
whisk together to make a smooth batter.

Pour approximately 1/3 cup batter for each pancake onto a hot
nonstick griddle or pan, using a ladle or large spoon. Turn the pancakes over when there are bubbles across the top and the edges are
beginning to brown. Pancakes should be golden brown, and will
spring back when touched.

## Variations

*Chocolate Chip Hotcakes:* Sprinkle 1 teaspoon mini chocolate chips
on each pancake after it has cooked for a few seconds on the first
side. (Cooking for a few seconds keeps the chips from sinking
through to the bottom.) It is helpful to use a small spoon to press
them into the batter. Continue to cook as directed.

*Zesty Orange Hotcakes:* Add 2 tablespoons grated orange peel and
2 tablespoons orange juice to the wet ingredients. Cook as directed.

*Spiced Pancakes:* Add 1/4 teaspoon each of ground cinnamon,
ground allspice, ground nutmeg, and ground ginger to the dry ingredients. Cook as directed.

*Cornmeal Hotcakes:* Replace 1/4 cup of the flour with 1/4 cup masa,
and add to the dry ingredients. Add 1 tablespoon honey to the wet
ingredients.

*Cinnamon Raisin Hotcakes:* Add 1 teaspoon ground cinnamon and ⅓ cup chopped raisins to the dry ingredients. Cook as directed.

*Multigrain Hotcakes:* Replace ½ cup of all-purpose flour with ¼ cup whole wheat flour and ¼ cup oat flour. Add to the dry ingredients. Cook as directed.

### Each Serving Provides

164 Calories, 21% from Fat, 4 g Fat, 25 g Carbohydrates, 6 g Protein,
122 mg Calcium, 1 g Dietary Fiber, 323 mg Sodium, 32 mg Cholesterol.

# German Apple Pancakes

Here is my lowfat rendition of an old favorite. The apples are
chopped smaller than in the traditional version and cooked
before they go into the batter, making them tender and delicious.
The flavor is enhanced by just the right amount of cinnamon
for a melt-in-your-mouth breakfast treat.

**8 pancakes**

| | | | |
|---|---|---|---|
| 1 | medium-sized Granny Smith apple, peeled, cored, and coarsely chopped in a food processor | 1 | tablespoon baking powder |
| | | $1/2$ | teaspoon salt |
| | | 1 | teaspoon cinnamon |
| | | 1 | cup lowfat buttermilk |
| $1/4$ | cup granulated sugar | $1/2$ | cup 2 percent milk |
| 1 | teaspoon fresh lemon juice | 1 | large whole egg |
| $1/2$ | cups all-purpose flour | 1 | tablespoon canola oil |
| 3 | tablespoons granulated sugar | 1 | tablespoon vanilla extract |

In a small saucepan combine the chopped apples, $1/4$ cup sugar,
and lemon juice. Cook over high heat until apples are tender and
all the liquid has evaporated. Set aside to cool.

In a large mixing bowl combine flour, sugar, baking powder, salt,
and cinnamon. In a separate mixing bowl combine all remaining ingredients, including the apples, and whisk together until smooth.
Pour into dry ingredients and whisk until all ingredients are well
combined. This will be a thick and rather bumpy-looking batter.

Pour approximately $1/2$ cup batter for each pancake onto a hot,
nonstick griddle or pan, using a ladle or large spoon. These pancakes are meant to look uneven and bumpy, but you may want to
spread the batter out a bit with a spoon once it is on the griddle.

Turn the pancakes over when there are bubbles across the top
and the edges are beginning to brown. These tend to brown a bit
faster than other hotcakes so watch them closely. Pancakes should
be golden brown and will spring back when touched.

### Each Serving Provides

189 Calories, 16% from Fat, 3 g Fat, 34 g Carbohydrates, 5 g Protein,
88 mg Calcium, 1 g Dietary Fiber, 307 mg Sodium, 30 mg Cholesterol.

# Banana Hotcakes

## 8 hotcakes

1 cup all-purpose flour
½ cup whole wheat flour
2 tablespoons granulated sugar
1 tablespoon baking powder
½ teaspoon salt
½ teaspoon ground allspice
½ teaspoon ground cinnamon

1 cup lowfat buttermilk
1 medium-sized ripe banana, mashed (approx. ½ cup)
½ cup plus 1 tablespoon 2 percent milk
1 large whole egg
1 tablespoon canola oil
2 teaspoons vanilla extract

In a large mixing bowl combine both flours, sugar, baking powder, salt, and spices. In a food processor combine buttermilk and banana, and process until smooth. Pour into a separate mixing bowl and add 2 percent milk, egg, oil, and vanilla. Whisk together until smooth and pour into dry ingredients. Whisk together to make a smooth batter.

Pour approximately ⅓ cup plus 1 tablespoon of batter (or just over ⅓ cup) onto hot griddle or pan, using a ladle or large spoon. Turn the hotcakes over when there are bubbles across the top and the edges are beginning to brown. Hotcakes should be golden brown and will spring back when touched.

## Variation

Try Chocolate Chip Banana Hotcakes! Sprinkle 1 teaspoon mini chocolate chips on each pancake after it has cooked for a few seconds on the first side. (Cooking for a few seconds keeps the chips from sinking through to the bottom.) It is helpful to use a small spoon to press them into the batter. Continue to cook as directed.

### Each Serving Provides

161 Calories, 19% from Fat, 4 g Fat, 27 g Carbohydrates, 5 g Protein, 91 mg Calcium, 2 g Dietary Fiber, 309 mg Sodium, 30 mg Cholesterol.

# Basic Buttermilk Waffle

For those of you who insist on having waffles,
look no further. These are crisp and light, ready to be
smothered in whatever topping your heart desires,
from maple syrup to luscious fruit toppings!

**12 four-inch waffles**

1 1/2 cups all-purpose flour
2 teaspoons baking powder
1/2 teaspoon salt
2 tablespoons granulated
   sugar
1 cup lowfat buttermilk

1/2 cup 2 percent milk
1 large whole egg
1 tablespoon canola oil
2 teaspoons vanilla extract
2 large egg whites, room temperature

In a large mixing bowl combine flour, baking powder, salt, and sugar. In a separate mixing bowl combine all remaining ingredients except for the two egg whites, and whisk together until smooth. Pour into dry ingredients and whisk together to make a smooth batter.

In a small mixing bowl beat the egg whites with an electric mixer until firm peaks form. Carefully fold beaten egg whites into batter using a rubber spatula.

Pour approximately 1/3 cup batter for each waffle into a hot waffle iron. (This measurement is based on a 4 × 4-inch waffle; you may need to adjust amount for your waffle iron.) Cook until waffles are crisp and golden brown.

## Variations

Of course this recipe is delicious on its own, but do try these delicious variations, too. It's easy to add any number of different ingredients to this basic batter for some exciting new waffle flavors!

*Cornmeal-Orange Waffles:* Substitute 1/4 cup masa for 1/4 cup of the flour, and add 1 1/2 tablespoons grated orange peel. Cook as directed. These are delicious with Blueberry Topping (page 130) and light whipped cream.

*Cinnamon Raisin Waffles:* Add 1 1/2 teaspoons ground cinnamon and 1/2 cup chopped raisins to the dry ingredients. Cook as directed. Try these with Cinnamon Syrup (page 125) or even Sun-Dried Cherry Syrup (page 128).

*Belgian Hazelnut Waffles:* Add 1/3 cup finely ground toasted hazelnuts to the dry ingredients, and 1 1/2 tablespoons hazelnut liqueur to the wet ingredients. Cook as directed. My first choice with these is Cinnamon Syrup (page 125); however, they are awfully tasty when paired up with Chunky Strawberry Topping (page 129) and some light whipped cream.

*Whole Wheat Waffles:* Substitute 1/2 cup whole wheat flour for 1/2 cup of the all-purpose flour. Add 1 tablespoon honey to the wet ingredients. Cook as directed.

*Lemon Poppy-Seed Waffles:* Add an additional 2 tablespoons granulated sugar, 1 1/2 tablespoons poppy seeds, and 1 tablespoon grated lemon peel to the dry ingredients. Add 1 tablespoon fresh lemon juice to the wet ingredients. Cook as directed. Serve these with Raspberry Syrup (page 123) just as you would the Lemon Poppy-Seed Hotcakes.

### Each Serving Provides

101 Calories, 18% from Fat, 2 g Fat, 16 g Carbohydrates, 4 g Protein,
49 mg Calcium, 0 g Dietary Fiber, 185 mg Sodium, 18 mg Cholesterol.

# Syrups, Toppings, and Spreads

**Waking** up to a breakfast of piping hot scones, luscious muffins, or a stack of fluffy flapjacks is already a special thing, so what could possibly make it better? How about some caramel pecan syrup drizzling down that stack of hotcakes? Maybe that muffin would like a swipe of cranberry cream cheese. And then there's that scone, just dreaming of being filled with your favorite flavor of jam. Whatever floats your boat, you're sure to find the perfect finishing touch in the pages of this chapter. I urge you to be adventuresome and try the different flavored syrups with your pancakes; you might end up liking some of them even better than always having maple! And by all means, try the special butters and flavored cream cheeses on bagels, toast, or English muffins as well as the muffins in this book.

# Raspberry Syrup

What could be more delicious than rich, red syrup, bursting with
fresh raspberry flavor, oozing down your stack of hotcakes or
generously filling up every little hole in your golden crisp waffle?
This raspberry syrup is a treat for the eye as well as the palate.
Move over, maple syrup, times are changing!

**8 servings of 3 tablespoons each**

2 cups frozen, unsweetened
   raspberries
1 cup water
³/₄ cup granulated sugar

¹/₄ teaspoon butter or mar-
   garine (reduces foaming
   during cooking)
¹/₂ cup light corn syrup

In a medium-sized saucepan combine the berries and the water.
Cook over high heat for approximately 10 minutes, breaking up
the berries as they cook, using a wire whisk. Cool for 10 minutes
and then strain through a fine-mesh sieve, using a large spoon or
ladle to push through as much of the juice and pulp as possible.
You should end up with 1 ¹/₂ cups. If you are a bit shy of that
amount, add enough water to bring it up to the correct amount.

Return the liquid to a clean, medium-sized saucepan and whisk
in the sugar and butter. Place over high heat and cook for 10 minutes, or until temperature reaches 200 degrees on a candy thermometer. Remove from heat and whisk in corn syrup.

Cool syrup completely and store in an airtight container in the
refrigerator.

*When this syrup cools, it will thicken almost to the consistency of a soft jelly
because of the pectin in the berries. Before serving, warm it in the microwave
for a few seconds or over the stove in a small saucepan.*

### Each Serving Provides

140 Calories, 2% from Fat, 0 g Fat, 37 g Carbohydrates, 0 g Protein,
8 mg Calcium, 1 g Dietary Fiber, 26 mg Sodium, 0 mg Cholesterol.

Syrups, Toppings, and Spreads

# Caramel Pecan Syrup

This delicately flavored syrup offers a light version of a classic combination. Its caramel toffee taste and crunchy toasted pecans go perfectly with pancakes and waffles.

**5 servings of approximately 3 tablespoons each**

½ cup brown sugar, firmly
    packed
½ teaspoon salt
½ cup water

½ cup light corn syrup
1 teaspoon butter-flavored
    extract
⅓ cup chopped toasted pecans

In a medium-sized saucepan combine brown sugar, salt, and water. Place over high heat and cook undisturbed for 5 minutes or until a candy thermometer reads 200 degrees. The mixture will thicken to a syrupy consistency. Be careful not to caramelize the sugar, which can happen rather quickly at this stage.

    Remove from heat and stir in remaining ingredients. Cool completely and store in an airtight container in the refrigerator.

*Serve this syrup at room temperature or, for a real treat, warm it in the microwave for a few seconds or over the stove in a small saucepan.*

### Each Serving Provides

232 Calories, 20% from Fat, 5 g Fat, 49 g Carbohydrates, 1 g Protein,
24 mg Calcium, 1 g Dietary Fiber, 262 mg Sodium, 0 mg Cholesterol.

# Cinnamon Syrup

If you like cinnamon, this syrup is for you. Light,
luscious, and full of fresh cinnamon flavor, it is a delicious
alternative, especially on hazelnut waffles!

**5 servings of approximately 3 tablespoons each**

| | |
|---|---|
| 1 cup water | ½ cup light corn syrup |
| 2 cinnamon sticks | 1 tablespoon dark corn syrup |
| ½ cup granulated sugar | ½ teaspoon ground cinnamon |

In a medium-sized saucepan combine the water and cinnamon
sticks. Place over high heat and cook until liquid is reduced by half
and has turned light brown from the cinnamon, approximately 10
minutes. Leaving the cinnamon sticks in the pan, stir in the sugar,
clip a candy thermometer to the side of the pan, and continue to
cook over high heat for approximately 5 minutes more or until the
candy thermometer reads 200 degrees. The mixture will thicken to
a syrupy consistency. Be careful not to caramelize the sugar, which
at this stage can happen rather quickly.

Remove from heat and stir in the remaining ingredients. Stirring with a whisk will disperse the cinnamon more easily.

Cool completely and store in an airtight container, leaving the
cinnamon sticks in the syrup.

*Serve at room temperature.*

### Each Serving Provides

173 Calories, 0% from Fat, 0 g Fat, 47 g Carbohydrates, 0 g Protein,
6 mg Calcium, 0 g Dietary Fiber, 45 mg Sodium, 0 mg Cholesterol.

Syrups, Toppings, and Spreads

# Vanilla Bean Syrup

Have you ever had vanilla ice cream made with real vanilla beans—
the kind where you can see the tiny little vanilla seeds? If so,
you know that the flavor of real vanilla beans is unmatched
by any extract. Oh that flavor! This syrup will have the same
effect on you when you drown your flapjacks in it.

**5 servings of approximately 3 tablespoons each**

| | |
|---|---|
| 1 cup water | $^1/_2$ cup light corn syrup |
| 1 vanilla bean | 1 tablespoon dark corn syrup |
| $^1/_2$ cup granulated sugar | |

Place the water in a medium-sized saucepan. Using a small, sharp
paring knife, split the vanilla bean in half, and use the blade of the
knife or the back of your thumbnail to scrape as many seeds as possible into the water. Then toss in the pod as well. Cook over high
heat, using a whisk to help break up the seeds. They will remain
clumped together until the mixture has thickened, whereupon
they will disperse throughout the syrup. Cook until liquid is reduced by half and is lightly tinted by the vanilla bean, approximately 10 minutes.

Stir in the sugar, leaving the bean in the pan, and continue to
cook over high heat for approximately 5 minutes more or until a
candy thermometer reads 200 degrees. The mixture will thicken to
a syrupy consistency. Be careful not to caramelize the sugar, which
at this stage can happen rather quickly.

Remove from heat and stir in the remaining ingredients using a whisk. Now the little vanilla seeds should be floating harmoniously throughout the syrup. Leave the pod in since it will continue to flavor the syrup.

Cool completely and store in an airtight container in the refrigerator.

*You may serve syrup at room temperature or warmed in the microwave for a couple of seconds. You can also warm it in a small saucepan over the stove.*

### Each Serving Provides

173 Calories, 0% from Fat, 0 g Fat, 47 g Carbohydrates, 0 g Protein,
3 mg Calcium, 0 g Dietary Fiber, 45 mg Sodium, 0 mg Cholesterol.

Syrups, Toppings, and Spreads

# Sun-Dried Cherry Syrup

Fruit syrups, such as boysenberry or strawberry, are a refreshing and light change from maple syrup. With its tart sun-dried cherries, you'll find this one particularly inviting. Sun-dried cherries usually come in two varieties: Royal Anne, which are more tart, and Bing, which are richer, darker, and sweeter. Buy either kind depending on what you're in the mood for.

**8 servings of approximately 3 tablespoons each**

| | |
|---|---|
| 1 cup water | ½ cup light corn syrup |
| ½ cup sun-dried cherries | 2 tablespoons dark corn |
| ½ cup granulated sugar | syrup |

In a medium-sized saucepan combine the water and cherries. Place over high heat and cook until cherries are tender and have absorbed half of the liquid, approximately 10 minutes. Stir in the sugar, leaving the cherries in the pan, and continue to cook over high heat for 5 more minutes or until a candy thermometer reads 200 degrees. Be careful not to caramelize the sugar, which at this stage it can happen rather quickly. Remove from heat and stir in the remaining ingredients.

Cool completely and store in an airtight container in the refrigerator.

*You may serve syrup at room temperature or warm it by heating in the microwave for a couple of seconds or over the stove in a small saucepan.*

## Hint

This syrup is also delicious when combined with other flavors such as a teaspoon of almond or vanilla extract.

### Each Serving Provides

140 Calories, 1% from Fat, 0 g Fat, 37 g Carbohydrates, 1 g Protein, 10 mg Calcium, 1 g Dietary Fiber, 32 mg Sodium, 0 mg Cholesterol.

# Chunky Strawberry Topping

This topping is made with fresh strawberries and is absolutely divine over a crisp waffle with some light whipped topping!

**8 servings of ¼ cup each**

| | |
|---|---|
| 1 pint fresh ripe strawberries, washed, hulled, and cut into ½-inch chunks | 2 teaspoons grated lemon peel |
| ¼ cup fresh orange juice | ¼ cup granulated sugar |
| ¼ cup water | 1 tablespoon cornstarch dissolved in 1 tablespoon cold water |
| 1 teaspoon fresh lemon juice | |
| 1 teaspoon fresh lime juice | |

In a medium-sized saucepan combine strawberries, orange juice, water, lemon juice, lime juice, lemon peel, and sugar. Cook over high heat until mixture reaches a boil. Continue to cook for 1 minute, stirring occasionally; then add dissolved cornstarch and stir to distribute. Continue to cook for another 30 seconds, stirring constantly. Mixture will have thickened.

Cool completely and store in an airtight container in the refrigerator.

*You may serve topping cold or warm it by heating in the microwave for a few seconds or over the stove in a small saucepan.*

### Each Serving Provides

41 Calories, 3% from Fat, 0 g Fat, 11 g Carbohydrates, 0 g Protein, 7 mg Calcium, 1 g Dietary Fiber, 1 mg Sodium, 0 mg Cholesterol.

Syrups, Toppings, and Spreads

# Blueberry Topping

Of all the fruits I ate as a child, I would have to say that I enjoyed blueberries—in pie—the most. I recall standing on my tiptoes to peek over the counter where the blueberry pie was kept. This blueberry topping will bring back any wonderful blueberry memories that you may have. It is as delicious on waffles as it is on hotcakes.

**8 servings of ¼ cup each**

1½ cups blueberries, fresh or frozen
½ cup water
3 tablespoons fresh orange juice
1 tablespoon fresh lemon juice

1 teaspoon grated lemon peel
2 teaspoons grated orange peel
¼ cup granulated sugar
1 tablespoon cornstarch dissolved in 1 tablespoon cold water

Combine all ingredients, except for cornstarch, in a medium-sized saucepan and cook over high heat, stirring occasionally, just until mixture comes to a boil. Continue to cook for 30 seconds; then add the dissolved cornstarch, stirring to distribute, and cook for an additional 30 seconds, stirring constantly but gently so the berries won't break. Mixture will have thickened.

Cool completely and store in an airtight container in the refrigerator.

*You may serve topping cold or warm it by heating in the microwave for a few seconds or over the stove in a small saucepan.*

### Each Serving Provides

44 Calories, 2% from Fat, 0 g Fat, 11 g Carbohydrates, 0 g Protein, 11 mg Calcium, 1 g Dietary Fiber, 1 mg Sodium, 0 mg Cholesterol.

# Sun-Dried Cherry Butter

After I created the sun-dried cherry syrup, I just couldn't stop myself! I had to devise a way of pairing that delectable taste with muffins and breads as well. This spread is great for topping off those muffins. It is also perfect for melting over your hotcakes.

**18 servings of 1 tablespoon each**

| | |
|---|---|
| ½ cup sun-dried cherries | ½ cup (4 ounces) light butter, |
| ½ cup water | room temperature |
| 2 tablespoons granulated | ¼ cup regular unsalted butter, |
| sugar | room temperature |

In a small saucepan combine cherries and water. Cook over high heat until cherries are plump and tender, and liquid has completely reduced to a thick, syrupy consistency. Be sure to stir it often and watch closely so it doesn't caramelize. Set cherries aside to cool completely.

When cherries have cooled, place them in a food processor along with the remaining ingredients and process to combine, scrape down the sides of the bowl as necessary. Butter will not be smooth, it should have chunks of cherries dispersed through it.

Store in an airtight container in the refrigerator.

### Each Serving Provides

62 Calories, 78% from Fat, 5 g Fat, 4 g Carbohydrates, 1 g Protein,
4 mg Calcium, 0 g Dietary Fiber, 32 mg Sodium, 16 mg Cholesterol.

# Apple Raisin Butter

This is a chunky and very fruity concoction that is not
only perfect for topping your muffins and breakfast
breads but for melting over hotcakes as well.

**16 servings of 1 tablespoon each**

½ cup dried apples
¼ cup sultanas
½ cup water
1 tablespoon granulated
  sugar
4 tablespoons light butter,
  room temperature

2 tablespoons regular
  unsalted butter, room
  temperature
¾ teaspoon ground cinnamon

In a medium-sized saucepan combine apples, sultanas, and water,
and cook over high heat, partially covered, until fruit is tender and
liquid has been absorbed. Set aside to cool completely.

When fruit has cooled, place it in a food processor and process
until it is chopped roughly. Add remaining ingredients and process
to bring the butter together, stopping occasionally to scrape down
the sides. The butter will be chunky in appearance.

Store in an airtight container in the refrigerator.

## Each Serving Provides

44 Calories, 63% from Fat, 3 g Fat, 5 g Carbohydrates, 0 g Protein,
4 mg Calcium, 0 g Dietary Fiber, 21 mg Sodium, 9 mg Cholesterol.

# Fig Butter

The poor little fig . . . I don't think it gets the attention it deserves. Figs are not only wonderfully delicious, they're good for you, too. They're an excellent source of fiber. Of course, we all love Fig Newtons, but for most of us that's as far as it goes. Well not anymore! This fig butter will completely change the way you feel about figs. It is sweet and rich with an unusual flavor that you can't seem to get enough of . . . kind of like those Fig Newtons!

**10 servings of 1 tablespoon each**

8  soft dried figs, stems removed, and chopped
1/2  cup (4 ounces) light butter, room temperature
2  tablespoons regular unsalted butter, room temperature

1  tablespoon brown sugar
1/2  teaspoon vanilla extract
1/4  teaspoon ground allspice

Combine all ingredients in a food processor and process to combine. This is a thick butter so you may have to stop the machine often to scrape down the sides of the bowl. The butter will be chunky in appearance when done.

Store in an airtight container in the refrigerator.

## Variation

For Fig Cream Cheese, substitute 4 ounces (1/2 cup) light Neufchâtel cheese for the butters.

### Each Serving Provides

108 Calories, 62% from Fat, 7 g Fat, 12 g Carbohydrates, 1 g Protein, 25 mg Calcium, 2 g Dietary Fiber, 59 mg Sodium, 23 mg Cholesterol.

# Spiced Butter

With its simple combination of brown sugar and spices,
this butter is easy to prepare to add some spur-of-the-moment
festivity to any of your muffins or breads.

**12 servings of 1 tablespoon each**

½ cup (4 ounces) light butter,
room temperature
¼ cup regular unsalted butter,
room temperature
2 tablespoons brown sugar

¾ teaspoon each:
ground cinnamon
ground cloves
ground cardamom
ground nutmeg
½ teaspoon vanilla extract

Combine all ingredients in a food processor and process until smooth, stopping occasionally to scrape down the bowl.

Store in an airtight container in the refrigerator.

## Variation

For Spiced Cream Cheese, substitute 6 ounces (¾ cup) light Neufchâtel cheese for the butters.

### Each Serving Provides

81 Calories, 91% from Fat, 8 g Fat, 3 g Carbohydrates, 1 g Protein,
6 mg Calcium, 0 g Dietary Fiber, 49 mg Sodium, 24 mg Cholesterol.

# Date Nut Cream Cheese

The chewy sweet dates and crunchy pecans make this spread a bit richer than the others, but the flavors go together beautifully. If you're a bagel eater, you won't want to miss this one.

**28 servings of 1 tablespoon each**

8 whole dates, pitted and chopped

4 ounces ($\frac{1}{2}$ cup) light Neufchâtel cheese, room temperature

2 tablespoons brown sugar

$\frac{1}{2}$ teaspoon vanilla extract

$\frac{1}{4}$ teaspoon ground allspice

2 tablespoons chopped toasted pecans

In a food processor combine chopped dates, Neufchâtel cheese, and brown sugar. Process for approximately 30 seconds to break up the dates. Then add remaining ingredients and process to combine, stopping occasionally to scrape down the bowl. Cheese will have a chunky texture.

Store in an airtight container in the refrigerator.

### Each Serving Provides

25 Calories, 48% from Fat, 1 g Fat, 3 g Carbohydrates, 1 g Protein,
5 mg Calcium, 0 g Dietary Fiber, 16 mg Sodium, 3 mg Cholesterol.

Syrups, Toppings, and Spreads

# Cranberry Orange Cream Cheese

Throughout this book, I have made a point of reminding people
to stock up on cranberries when they're in season. So if you
haven't done so already, throw a few bags in the freezer,
because when summer rolls around you will definitely want
to make this wonderful cream cheese. It's the perfect
spread for those lazy summer mornings.

**16 servings of 1 tablespoon each**

½ cup cranberries, fresh or
  frozen
¼ cup water
¼ cup granulated sugar
6 ounces (¾ cup) light
  Neufchâtel cheese

1 tablespoon granulated
  sugar
1 tablespoon grated orange
  peel

In a small saucepan combine cranberries, water, and ¼ cup sugar
and cook over high heat until the cranberries begin to pop. Continue to cook, stirring constantly, until liquid is completely reduced
and mixture is thick. Watch very closely as it can burn easily at this
stage. Set aside to cool completely.

When cranberry mixture is cool, place in a food processor with
remaining ingredients and process to combine, stopping occasionally to scrape down the bowl. Cheese will have a chunky texture.

Store in an airtight container in the refrigerator.

### Each Serving Provides

44 Calories, 52% from Fat, 3 g Fat, 5 g Carbohydrates, 1 g Protein,
9 mg Calcium, 0 g Dietary Fiber, 43 mg Sodium, 8  mg Cholesterol.

# Apricot Almond Cream Cheese

I happen to love the taste of tart dried apricots. So it
seemed very fitting to pair them up with crunchy toasted
almonds to make this heavenly cream cheese spread.

**12 servings of 1 tablespoon each**

8   small dried apricots
½   cup water
1   tablespoon granulated
    sugar
4   ounces (½ cup) light
    Neufchâtel cheese, room
    temperature

1   tablespoon granulated
    sugar
2   tablespoons chopped
    toasted almonds
1   teaspoon grated orange
    peel

In a small saucepan combine the apricots and water, and cook over
medium-high heat, partially covered, until apricots are tender and
liquid has been absorbed, approximately 10 to 15 minutes. Set
aside to cool completely.

When apricots have cooled, place them in a food processor
along with the remaining ingredients, and process to combine,
stopping occasionally to scrape down the bowl. Cheese will have a
chunky texture.

Store in an airtight container in the refrigerator.

### Each Serving Provides

46 Calories, 55% from Fat, 3 g Fat, 5 g Carbohydrates, 1 g Protein,
12 mg Calcium, 0 g Dietary Fiber, 38 mg Sodium, 7 mg Cholesterol.

# INDEX

Index

Index